JOCELYN KUHN

THROUGH
TRANSITIONS

A PRACTICAL GUIDE FOR
TURNING LIFE'S CHALLENGES
INTO OPPORTUNITIES TO *THRIVE*

DEDICATION

This book is dedicated to my Parents. Thank you for always believing in me, pushing me, and loving me.

ACKNOWLEDGMENTS

There are countless people who've had an incredible impact on my life and on this book. In fact, I probably could have written an entire book called *Acknowledgments for Thriving Through Transitions*. There is no way to adequately thank ALL the people who've had a profound impact on me, but I want to, at the very least, acknowledge the ones who've played the biggest role in my life and this book. The words within the following pages would have never found their way off of my computer and onto the page had it not been for some amazing people who helped me with countless hours of editing, formatting, re-editing, and so on.

I have to start by thanking my husband, Jason. Thank you for always being my rock, providing our family with stability and strength, believing in my crazy ideas, and always being my number one fan. I thank God for the night we met. I never knew what it was like to feel loved and cherished until I met you. I love you more.

To my kids–Kali, Landon and Baylor–thank you for being the light of my life. Thank you for pushing me to become the best version of myself I can. Thank you for helping me grow. I'll love you forever, I'll like you for always, and you know you'll always be my babies.

Mom, thank you for believing in me. Thank you for supporting me. Thank you for inspiring me. I love you so much and feel so incredibly blessed that I get to be your daughter. You are my best friend, and I strive to be more like you every day. Your strength, forgiveness, and optimistic outlook on life are truly remarkable.

Dad, thank you for teaching me so much in the 22 years I was blessed to have you here, in the physical realm. Thank you for continuing to teach me many years after your death. Thank you for pushing me as a child. Thank you for disciplining me. Thank you for making me write papers, read good books, and listen to Tony Robbins when we'd drive somewhere in your car. Thank you for helping me to learn forgiveness. Thank you for teaching me to take 100% responsibility for my life. I could think of a million things to thank you for, but most of all, thank you for loving me. I love you and miss you so much.

To all my siblings—Jordan, Jared, Janessa, and Jacob—thank you for being you! I love you all very much! Thank you for loving me, supporting me and giving me shit from time to time too. Life wouldn't be the same without you guys!

Grandma Barb and Grandpa Ray, thank you for always supporting me and all of us grandkids. Thank you for being the kind of people who endured incredible hardships and chose to thrive. Thank you for the incredible memories I'll cherish forever, of visiting you on the farm. Thank you for being pillars in your community, and for inspiring in me the desire to make my own, unique contribution to the world. Thank you for creating an amazing marriage and legacy for our family. You'll probably never know how much I look up to the two of you in every way.

Grandma Jeannie, thank you for being such a great example of someone who loved unconditionally. Thank you for our long talks about all the important stuff in life. Thank you for the many, many conversations we had after Dad died. I'm so glad you get to be with your baby boy now. I know you two are probably having a party up there!

Grandpa Gene and Kathy, thank you for always being a joyful presence in my life. I still love thinking about your big, sparkly smile from time to time. You always made the best sourdough biscuits, and I have fond memories of camping, staying with you and Kathy sometimes when I was younger, and getting together for dinners and celebrations as I got older.

I'd also like to thank my Step-Dad, Greg. Thank you for loving all of us kids through the death of our Dad. Thank you for loving Mom so deeply and being there with her through her accident. Thank you for being a great Grandpa to my children. I love you.

To my two bonus siblings, Kristy and Lane, thank you for being part of my life. I feel incredibly grateful that God brought each of you into my life when He did. Thank you for all the memories we've been blessed to share. I love you both very much.

To the rest of my extended family–aunts, uncles, cousins, nieces and in-laws–I'm so thankful for the love and support you've shown me throughout the years. I have fond memories with all of you and feel blessed to have such a wonderful family.

To my amazing friends, and to the countless clients who've become great friends, thank you for supporting my dreams. Thank you for inspiring me. Thank you for sharing your stories and life with me. I'm eternally grateful that I've been blessed to have so many beautiful, kind-hearted friends, and I appreciate each of you immensely.

To my coaches, Joey, Jolynn, Jake, and Michelle, thank you for pushing me. Thank you for helping me realize my potential. Thank you for your never-ceasing belief in me. You've each made such a significant mark on my life, and I will be forever grateful for you.

To Isabelle, thank you for your friendship and for writing such a beautiful forward. Thank you for your support and encouragement as a fellow Thriver! Thank you for being such a beautiful example of someone who chose to rise above the painful experiences you've been through and live your best life! You're such an inspiration to so many, and I'm excited to continue to work together to make the world a more loving place! Love you girl!

To Diana, thank you for your vision for my brand and this book. Thank you for being THE BEST at what you do. Thank you for somehow always making me look 10X better on camera than I do in real life. Thank you for the countless hours you poured into designing and formatting the book. You are truly amazing! I appreciate you so very much! Thank you, thank you, thank you!

To Tyler and the entire team at Author's Unite, thank you for bringing this book to life. Thank you for the hours you've spent strategizing, marketing and answering my constant stream of questions.

Thank you to my editing geniuses–Madison, Susan and Noelle–I'd be lost without you. Thank you for being the catalyst for finally completing this work. Thank you for your attention to detail, and for the hours spent reading and editing with a perfectionistic eye.

Thank you to my many mentors and teachers, the people whose lives have had an incredible impact on me from the self-development world: Tony Robbins, Jack Canfield, Rhonda Byrne, Oprah Winfrey, Mother Teresa, Gabrielle Bernstein, Danielle LaPorte, Lewis Howes, Cheryl Strayed, Eckhart Tolle, Stephen Covey, Tim Ferris, Dave Asprey, Robin Sharma, and Brian Johnson—just to name a few—thank you for inspiring me! Thank you for leading the way for others, like myself, who are determined to use their gifts and talents to add value to the world.

To my coaching clients and the companies I've been blessed to work with, thank you for your support of me and my work. I consider it a great privilege and honor to get to work with each of you and support you through your transitions.

Lastly, to you, the reader—thank you for allowing me to come along with you on your transitional journey. You are the reason for my fulfillment and passion, and I am forever grateful for you. Let's continue connecting. I would love to know more about you and your story. Let's connect on Facebook through the *Thriving Through Transitions Community*. I'd love to provide ongoing support as you navigate life's challenges. I'd love to support your THRIVING story. May you be blessed and experience all of the abundance that lies on the other side of thriving through your transitions.

FORWARD

by Isabel Sofia

If there is one thing I would tell my adolescent self, it is that healthily grieving through trauma and loss is important, and the longer you try to put it off, avoid it, or stuff your feelings down, the more that trauma will dig its way into every area of your life. The first real change in my life happened when I was thirteen and my Parent's divorce was finalized. That is when I realized that I would have to embrace this new reality, because the idealistic view of my life—that my Parents would get back together, and we would all live happily ever after—was not going to happen. To successfully move on, I had to accept that.

In a way, however, this transition—one of the many I'd live through in my adolescence—started me on the path to coping with change and understanding it in ways that create more resilience and less resistance.

My Father and I used to go to the Oregon State Fair together every year as a tradition, and although our relationship had been strained due to their divorce, the Fair was a nice way for us to bond and spend quality time together. Every year it was the same, we would ride his motorcycle, eat at Subway, and then spend a casual evening at the Fair. On September 3rd, 2012, I assumed this year would be no different. When we arrived home that day, I had absolutely no idea my entire life was about to change.

It was 5:00 pm—I remember it vividly—as we pulled into my Mother's neighborhood, I received a phone call. It was my Mom, but she sounded hysterical. She asked me desperately when I would be home, and as we pulled up to the driveway right then, I responded with, "We just got here." That's when my Mother, a woman who I always saw as brave and sturdy life force, came trembling towards us from the front door, bellowing words I never thought I would hear, "Your Brother is dead."

Within seconds, my whole world was spinning. I can recall shaking and walking backwards into the street, unable to process what was unraveling before me. My Grandmother hurried to comfort me, but I could not help but scream the word 'No' over and over again. Just like that, my life was flipped completely upside down and there was nothing I could do about it.

As one can imagine, the next few weeks were all a blur for my family and me. We were faced with a drastic change that none of us knew how to handle. What was once our reality was no longer ours. Everything was different. My brother, Tomas, was gone from this earthly realm and I would never see him again. This loss is the kind that shakes you to your core—every inch of your perspective is shifted into something new. Once you step foot into this new way of seeing things, a new you has developed and you must learn how to grow in order to move gracefully through the transition in your life. I was only fifteen-years-old when this happened, and suddenly I felt as though I'd aged overnight and morphed into someone I hardly recognized.

To give some background, I was raised in a rural town by the name of Helvetia, Oregon. I attended a small school called West Union Elementary, and the people we met through that school became our community. One family in particular was pivotal in my upbringing. The Mast family—a big family with gracious hearts—became one of those close connections my family would keep with us for the rest of our lives. Growing up, I spent a great deal of time at the Mast home and made so many memories there. This lead to my friendships with Jocelyn Mast, now Kuhn, and her sister Janessa. As we grew, Jocelyn and I formed a bond that would sustain me through a lot of my healing over the years.

Only two years after my brother passed away, my Mother lost her battle with cancer, forcing me to again face the dreaded transition process. That time, I did a lot of the grieving on my own. Jocelyn reached out and became kind of like a mentor to me during that time. She is one of those people with wisdom embedded in her soul; a sense of security within herself that most people struggle to find their entire lives. The way she handled challenging circumstances as a young adult with courage was always inspiring to me.

Although we did not see each other often, she made it clear she cared about me and what I was going through. After we would spend time together, I would find myself reflecting on the advice she gave me. It was always relevant to my current situation, and I would leave feeling encouraged and motivated to face my life confidently. She would tell me to look toward my future and give encouraging tips as to how to get there. It was during those brief moments that I realized Jocelyn was here on Earth to help people.

As somebody who has endured great loss, and faced many changes in life, Jocelyn's words in *Thriving Through Transitions* are poignant and profound to read. Every person processes these changes in their own unique way, and the tools in this book are intended to encourage anyone who has to face the transition process and help them do it in healthy ways as opposed to letting their circumstances rule their lives. Many of us fall victim to life and feel as though life just happens to us; attached to the feeling that we have little to no control over what goes on in our reality. This is what Jocelyn highlights so well–she understands the perspective but gently suggests another. While we do not have all of the control, we do have control of how we view the world. All of us are going to experience change in our lives–small or large–whether it be a new job, a move across the country, a heartbreaking loss or an end to a relationship. No matter who you are, positive coping mechanisms will be crucial to your success and adaptability.

In this book, you will be introduced to techniques and methods designed to encourage shifting the focus of your energy. In life, it is so easy to get caught up in the day-to-day that we forget to honor our emotions. Then years down the line we realized we never truly gave ourselves time to process what we were going through, let alone heal it.

After my Mother passed away four years ago, I found myself curious to try painting for the first time. It was the depression I felt from the loss of my Mother that lead me to the paintbrush and canvas–something I am eternally grateful for–which lead me to my currently booming career as an artist. Art became a healthy outlet for me to process all of the emotions I was feeling through such an immediate loss, especially so soon after the other loss I had faced only two years before.
There was a lot for me to work through. But painting was something that flowed through me once I changed my perspective on my circumstances and decided to thrive in my new environment instead of dwell in the past.

Meditation, yoga, and walking through the forest or on the beach are other ways I am able to harness my focus and be in the present moment. This way I can clearly see where I still need to check in with myself, what inner work still needs to be done, and ways I can continue moving forward. With change, comes anxiety. Living with anxiety has been a struggle for me, and as a little girl, I dreaded change of all kinds. As one can see, me spending countless hours worrying about what may happen did nothing to stop the deaths of two of my loved ones. And neither will worrying about what may happen in the future. We can always feel sorry for ourselves, or worry relentlessly, and sometimes those days will come, but overall, it is going to be much more empowering to walk through life using the cards you've been dealt rather than complaining about the one's you're lacking.

Thriving Through Transitions is for anyone who still has some healing to do, a seemingly daunting change ahead of them, or grief that will remain with them forever. In her life, she has faced hardships that have given her the experience to help others live their lives happily on the other side of change. Jocelyn Kuhn is living proof that anyone can thrive through life's transitions. Including you.

CONTENTS

Introduction

INTRODUCTION

"It is not the strongest of the species that survives, nor the most intelligent. It is the one that is the most adaptable to change." —Charles Darwin

As I woke up on October 27, 2007 it felt like an ordinary day. My Dad was staying with me and he and I had planned to go watch my little brother's football game that morning. My then-husband got up early to go to work. He made a pot of coffee, gathered his things, and as he left, yelled something to me about asking my Dad to turn off the TV before he goes bed in the future.

After lazily sipping my first cup of coffee, I got up and started getting my boys ready for all the activities of the day. Landon, my two-year-old, was eager to get to his uncle's game, so once he was ready, I told him to go downstairs and wake Grandpa who was still asleep on the couch. A few minutes later, he came back up and told me in his two-year-old, impatient tone that grandpa wouldn't wake up. I didn't think much of it but went to the bottom of the stairs and yelled for him. NOTHING.

I had jumped on the phone with my Mom to go over the day's events after sending Landon downstairs. I began yelling louder and as I yelled more and he wouldn't stir, I began to worry.

"Dad, wake up! Dad... DAD!

"Mom, Dad won't wake up. I think something's wrong!"

"Well, if you're really worried, call 911. I'm sure he's just fine. He probably took a pain killer for his back, and is groggy and slow to wake up," she said. He'd been suffering from some pretty severe back pain, so it wasn't out of the question.

Still, I persisted, "I don't think so. Something doesn't seem right. I'm going to call."

I hung up the phone and for the first time in my life I dialed the numbers, 9-1-1. Even as I did, I remember feeling completely silly. I've always been a worrier. I kept thinking, "He's going to wake up and be so pissed that I'm freaking out like this." My worries were soon interrupted by the voice on the other end of the line.

"9-1-1. What's your emergency?"

I could barely speak, and when I did, I started to lose it. I touched my Dad's hand. It was stiff and cold. Now, I really started freaking out. I was holding my younger son, Baylor, who had just turned one, in one arm, the phone in the other. The operator told me to move any objects that could be blocking his airway, and then she walked me through CPR while we waited for the ambulance.

All the while, I kept thinking, "This can't be happening. This has to be a nightmare. I can't handle anymore!"

At this point Baylor–seeing I was visibly upset–had started crying. Landon ran around screaming, wondering when we were going to go to the football game, not understanding the gravity of the situation. I was trying to simultaneously listen to the operator on the other end of the line over Landon's screams, hold and console my crying one-year-old, and move the pillow propped behind my Dad's head so I could somehow begin administering CPR–something I had never done before.

I touched his face. It was cold and stiff just like his arm, but this time, my worst fears set in. I started to cry. The operator told me to remain calm and begin CPR, but I just couldn't do it.

"I can't do it," I cried.

As I sat there in agony, my thoughts were quickly interrupted by the operator gently and carefully asking the most God-awful question I have ever been asked–one that no one ever wants to be asked.

"Do you think he's dead?" she asked.

As I sobbed on the phone, I couldn't bring myself to admit the worst. I just cried. Finally, she said, "Ma'am, why don't you head outside to meet the EMTs."

I grabbed the boys and went outside where medical services were finally arriving. They rushed past me, asking where my Dad was located. As I followed them in and back down the stairs, I caught a glimpse of the EMT's face from across the room. It was horrified. It was the kind of expression that only happens when you know there's nothing good coming next.

The rest of the EMTs began setting down their equipment, turning to one another with that same horrified look—a look that only those who are experienced in this type of thing would understand—it was as if their faces spoke a coded language for, "There's nothing we can do here."

At that same moment, or maybe moments later, I'm not exactly sure of the timeline now, I saw one of them mouth, "He's gone."

"Nooooooo!" My knees hit the floor, I dropped my son. All I could think was, "I can't breathe. I can't breathe, I can't fucking breathe!"

At 43-years-old, my Dad had made his exit from this world, and my four younger siblings and I were now fatherless.

I learned fairly early on in life about an inevitable truth, one that we start to experience at birth and continue to experience every day for the duration of our lives. No one has ever escaped this truth, and no matter how hard someone tries, they will never elude it: the inevitability that nothing ever remains the same. From the day you were born there has never been a single day that you have stopped transitioning from one stage to the next. Sure, sometimes the progress is so slow that it may seem like you're the same person today as you were yesterday, but did you know that the average adult produces 222-242 billion new cells EVERY DAY! Even while you sleep your body is naturally in the process of transition.

Writers and philosophers have spoken of this truth for centuries.

Lao Tzu, mystic, philosopher, and author of the *Tao Te Ching* stated more than two thousand years ago, "Life is a series of natural and spontaneous changes. Don't resist them; that only creates sorrow. Let reality be reality. Let things flow naturally forward in whatever way they like."

The great Gautama Buddha taught, "Every morning we are born again—what we do today is what matters most." He also talked of the inevitability of change, stating, "The world is afflicted by death and decay. But the wise do not grieve, having realized the nature of the world."

The *Bible* declares in Ecclesiastes 3:1, "For everything there is a season, and a time for every matter under heaven."

More recently, the late Stephen Hawking is attributed with the saying that, "Intelligence is the ability to adapt to change."

Countless quotes and stories from some of the wisest thought leaders throughout time all point to this truth, yet so many of us spend our lives trying to avoid it, as if somehow, we can freeze time and live only our favorite moments forever.

Why do we do this? Do we really think life can remain the same forever? And do we even realistically want things to stay the same? The obvious answer is no. When we find a partner and fall in love we happily say yes to marriage, moving in with them and changing everything about our previous reality. When we get accepted to the college of our dreams to study something that really interests us, it's usually not too hard to make that decision. The reason? We embrace and accept the changes we *want* with open arms. When we look ahead and perceive the good in a potential change or transition, the word that comes to mind instead of 'change' is GROWTH.

While growth can be challenging and difficult at times, the word GROWTH implies something much more positive than CHANGE. Think about it. Flowers grow. Babies grow. Businesses grow. And most people associate very positive feelings with growing.

But think about CHANGE. The weather is about to CHANGE. Your boss just sent out an email saying CHANGE is coming. Your boyfriend/girlfriend just texted saying they're wanting to make some CHANGES in the relationship. Positive or negative? Most people would say that the word change elicits a much more negative or, at best, neutral feeling than the word GROWTH, even though both words are really referencing the same thing.

GROWTH feels voluntary while CHANGE feels involuntary and, as a result, change can feel scary. Sometimes change punches us in the gut so hard we don't know how we'll get back up. We just want to lay there, lifeless and still, and hope that the storm will indeed pass. Unfortunately, that doesn't always happen. Sometimes we can't go back to the way things used to be. Sometimes we are left to pick up the pieces and learn to live life without the comfort of familiarity.

Sometimes we choose change, but many times change chooses us–experiencing the death of a loved one, getting laid off, coming to the end of a life stage, realizing a marriage or relationship is over, taking on a new role or giving one up–these are some great examples of those punch-in-the-gut moments in life. Some of these moments happen gradually, while other times our life changes in the blink of an eye.

Even change that we proactively seek–taking a promotion at work, leaving a toxic relationship, going back to school, moving to a new city, starting a family or beginning a new career–can be exciting and transformative, but it can also bring feelings of insecurity, doubt, and fear of the unknown.

While change can bring even the best of us to our knees, it doesn't have to keep us there. That's what *THRIVING THROUGH TRANSITIONS* is all about-not just surviving life but *thriving* through it. Not just experiencing CHANGE but choosing GROWTH. When you think about it, life's just a game of change. By choosing to grow (wiser, kinder, stronger, more directed) from our experiences we are able to leave the world a better place, touch the hearts of the people we love, and experience the happiness and joy that comes only from growing into the best version of ourselves we can become.

DEFINING YOUR
YOUR
Transition

FROM THE DAY YOU WERE BORN THERE HAS NEVER BEEN A SINGLE DAY THAT YOU HAVE STOPPED *transitioning* FROM ONE STAGE TO THE NEXT.

DEFINING YOUR TRANSITION

TRANSITION

Def:

1. *a: a passage from one state, stage, subject, or place to another: change*

   b: a movement, development, or evolution from one form, stage, or style to another

Any transition is by definition a movement from somewhere to somewhere else. Whether we've sought it out or it's thrust upon us; whether positive or negative, we lose things from the place we've left behind.

When parents suddenly lose a child, they can lose much of their identity. They might feel they've lost their purpose and a huge part of their own lives. They also might feel the loss of love and connection that their child brought them.

When a marriage ends, even if it was a bad marriage, former spouses can feel like they are losing their comfort and routine. The marriage could have provided them with a sense of security and certainty that they no longer feel.

A college student on the verge of graduating might feel excited at the prospect of completing their degree, yet may still feel anxiety or sadness at the idea of leaving friends and a familiar routine. One with a job locked in may still fear losing the relative freedom of student life. One without a clear plan may be afraid of leaving the well-structured environment of school.

The process of transitioning is like the line that connects two points on a map. When Point A is no longer an option (or in some cases, it's no longer the option you choose),

3

your transition is the in-between, the time in which you've left one stage of life and aren't yet to the next one. That's why change is scary. We feel the pain of no longer being able to return to our Point A. It pushes us outside of our comfort zone and sometimes it breaks us of our current identity. It can be painful and difficult, especially if Point A was a place we felt comfortable and happy.

Imagine leaving home (Point A) completely alone with only your necessities, a hundred dollars, and a plane ticket to a foreign land (Point B). You can't speak the language, you've given up all the comforts of home, and you have to find a way to survive. Could you do it? Of course you *could*. Would it be painful at times? Most definitely.

Each person has a different level of tolerance for the loss and inherent ambiguity of that transition time. But if, as Darwin surmises, only the most adaptable survive, by expanding our ability to handle change, we can greatly alter our lives. No one knows how they'll be able to deal with the blows of life until they have to, but miraculously, most of the time people surprise themselves with their ability to keep moving forward despite hardships. Some of us are even able to find the good in an otherwise terrible situation, and that's a big part of what I'll share with you in the following pages. I'm going to give you the tools to work through any transition with clarity and understanding so you can turn your darkest days into your greatest assets.

There are 5 Steps in every successful transition that, if taken thoughtfully and intentionally, will allow you to THRIVE. I've experienced some very significant transitions in my life, and these Steps have helped me conquer the fear of change over and over again.

But this wasn't always the case. I didn't always recognize or use these tools, and in fact, I stumbled upon them quite unknowingly. It was in my darkest moments, the moments where I started to question, "Why would God make me experience so much pain? What is the purpose of going through such difficult situations? Why does life seem so unfair?" that I stumbled upon these Steps. So, if you're thinking your ability to handle change is preset within you, I can assure you, it's not. I was the most anxiety-stricken kid you could imagine. I actually think I lost about a year's worth of sleep as a teen because I would lay awake thinking about all the bad things that could happen to me or my family. I would think about what would happen if I ever lost one of them. I would think about how scary it would be to be out on my own. If there was something bad on the news I would internalize it and think, 'that's going to happen to me next.' To say I was afraid of change is a sore understatement.

Today, I've worked to accept and embrace change with open arms. Some of those bad things *did* happen in my life, but by embracing these 5 Steps of *THRIVING THROUGH TRANSITIONS* I've been able to proactively walk through those hard times knowing change is an inevitable part of life. In fact, I'd even say, all of the seemingly terrible events in my life have really all been happening FOR me, not to me (more on that later).

As a Transitional Coach, I've had the privilege of helping countless people navigate through difficult transitions, and these 5 Steps have helped numerous clients walk through their own periods of growth and change. If you're reading this and you need help handling your own life transitions, I fully believe that these Steps will help you too.

Within each of the Steps, we'll work on building and growing your adaptability muscle, so you can come to ENJOY change. Whether you're someone who normally thrives on adventure, but you've been dealt a punch-in-the-gut moment, or you're someone who avoids change at all costs, I believe learning to THRIVE through the inevitability of change using the 5 Steps presented in this book will have an incredible impact on your ability to respond to change and choose GROWTH, no matter what life throws your way.

THE 5 STEPS TO THRIVING THROUGH TRANSITIONS:

GRIEVE
REFRAME
CENTER
CREATE
ACT

In this book we will work through these 5 Steps together. While we walk together, keep in mind: Nothing in life is rigid, and a one-size-fits-all approach never works. Allow your process to unfold in whatever way it needs to. You may find yourself realizing you need to go back to step one and deal with a loss you hadn't considered, or you may find that while creating your vision for the future, you end up needing to re-center in the present. THAT'S LIFE. There is no right or wrong.

Our lives are fluid and complicated. So *please*, don't beat yourself up feeling like you need to do everything in this program, exactly as it says or in order. LISTEN to your own inner wisdom and let it guide your THRIVING TRANSITION. Some people like to read a book and go through all the processes in each chapter as they read it, while others find it more appealing to read the full book and then go back and do the work in each section. Personally, I'm a big-picture thinker, so until I see how all the details come together, it's hard for me to understand why each step of a process is important. Whatever the case may be for you, let your own intuition be your guide.

I've designed this book with the intention of helping people with life's hardest moments, but it works for smaller transitions as well. Keep this in mind as you go through the Steps.

For example, when working through this process with a friend of mine recently, she identified that she'd really like to make some changes to her home life. Specifically, she wanted to become a more engaged mom. As we started to go through the process of THRIVING THROUGH TRANSITIONS there were certain portions that didn't fully apply to her situation. Mainly, she didn't feel the need to GRIEVE anything because nothing was really wrong; she just wanted things to be better.

While I agreed that her GRIEVE process wouldn't look like the grieving process of someone who had experienced the sudden loss of a loved one, I also pushed her to acknowledge some of the things she would need to sacrifice in order to become the mom she wanted to be. She was then able to identify several things she hadn't even realized she would be giving up to hit the goal she had of becoming a more engaged mom. She thought of things like limiting phone screen time in the evening to two 15-minute periods, cutting out 2 TV shows per week, and cutting back on drinking wine on weekdays. She understood she'd be forfeiting the sense of calm and relaxation that she normally felt during the evening when she'd drink her wine and watch her shows. Her "free" time would be depleted in order to prioritize her kids more, and she would miss out on the entertainment of watching her shows and getting caught up in the lives of the characters.

While she didn't really need to GRIEVE any of those losses in the way a person going through a traumatic life event would, it was valuable for her to identify that she was choosing to give up certain habits (Point A) to work toward something she wanted more (Point B).

If you can relate to my friend's story, my suggestion is to go through each of the Steps regardless of the magnitude of the transition you face.

I recently attended a conference called *Unleash the Power Within*, put on by Tony Robbins. Over the course of the 4-day weekend of growth and transformation, one of the key takeaways I heard from him over and over was that, "The quality of your life is determined by the quality of the questions you ask yourself on a consistent basis."

With this in mind, I have included plenty of high-quality, thought-provoking questions. It's in answering these questions for ourselves that we greatly increase the quality of our lives. If there are questions that don't pertain to you or your transition, skip them. Like I said earlier, don't read this book expecting a one-size-fits-all approach. If you're expecting that, you're going to be disappointed. This book is merely a guide, but ultimately your transition is uniquely your own and no one, including me, can tell you the exact steps you'll need to take to get from Point A to Point B.

That said, the Steps I'll share with you in the following pages will most likely help spark some ideas for you. There will be stories you can relate to, but the only way your life will start to change for the better is if you commit to answering the questions for yourself and fully engage in the process of THRIVING THROUGH YOUR OWN TRANSITION.

IDENTIFY THE TRANSITION

LET'S GET STARTED...

Before we begin the process of THRIVING THROUGH TRANSITIONS, let's first establish what exactly your transition is. Knowledge is power (or at least potential power), and nowhere is that knowledge more powerful than in the case of your own life. Through this exercise of identifying your transition in detail, you'll be able to move through the process with clarity and more thoroughly enjoy who you become along the way.

Think of the process of a caterpillar becoming a butterfly – if a butterfly were a butterfly from the beginning we probably wouldn't appreciate its splendor in the same way. There is something beautiful and inspiring about the transformation that takes a plain looking caterpillar and turns it into a magnificent butterfly. Our transformations and transitions in life are similar. They can give us a great sense of meaning and purpose, and of pride and satisfaction. They can be beautiful and inspire those around us.

For that to be the case, however, we need to know precisely where we are starting from and also, where we are going next. We need to know the nitty-gritty details like, "What am I giving up? What am I losing? What do I want now? What direction do I want to move in?"

In other words, we need to *define* our Point A and Point B. Then transition becomes as simple as connecting the line between the two. Just keep in mind Point B is simply another stop on the map and Point B will eventually give way to Point C, and D, and so on. For now though, let's clearly identify our Point A. We'll also briefly outline our Point B here, but we'll round this out in Step 4 when we create a clear and exciting vision for our future!

What is the transition I'm experiencing right now?

_____

_____

_____

_____

_____

_____

_____

_____

As I shift from the old to the new, what am I giving up and/or losing? Have I already experienced the loss, or am I fearing the loss that will need to take place in order to become the person I want to be?

_____

_____

_____

_____

_____

_____

_____

_____

_____

Where am I moving to? Where do I want to go from here?

_____

_____

_____

_____

_____

_____

_____

_____

_____

_____

*By definition a transition is a movement from one state/form/stage to another one, so it is absolutely crucial to KNOW WHERE YOU ARE GOING. We will talk more in depth about this when we get to Step 4, but for now, briefly summarize where you are headed or where you would like to be heading. Don't worry too much if you are stuck on this, just let your thoughts flow.

Often, especially with sudden loss, we have no idea where we want to head next. It's hard to identify a new and exciting reality when we had no desire for the change to happen in the first place. As we'll discuss later on, this is one of the reasons a sudden loss is often one of the most debilitating transitions we face—we usually don't have any idea of where we want to go next. It's hard to define our Point B because nothing seems like it could ever be as good as Point A was. If you find yourself in this type of transition, leave this blank for now. It's perfectly okay not to know where you want to go quite yet. This book is designed to help you find that Point B.

If you have a general idea of what you think you might want your Point B to look like, write it down. You may end up changing your mind as you work through the Steps, and that's okay. It's just another opportunity to show yourself how adaptable you really are.

LISTEN
TO YOUR
OWN INNER
WISDOM
AND LET IT
GUIDE YOUR
thriving
TRANSITION.

STEP 1

Grieve.

IN A WORLD
OF INSTANT
EVERYTHING,
IT'S HARD
TO ACCEPT
THAT
grieving
TAKES TIME.

STEP 1 - GRIEVE.
GRIEVE THE LOSS

"Grief is like the ocean; it comes on waves ebbing and flowing. Sometimes the water is calm, and sometimes it is overwhelming. All we can do is learn to swim." –Vicki Harrison

Whenever we move through a transition we are moving away from one thing and toward another, and that usually comes with the pain of loss. This is especially true of transitions that weren't part of our game plan (i.e. the unexpected layoff, the sudden death of a loved one, a spouse having an affair, etc.), but it can also be true when we are choosing to walk away from one thing and move toward something different. Sometimes we've come to the end of one stage of life, such as finishing college or retiring from our career, and we are simply giving up the comfort and security of our daily routine.

In any case, it's important to look at the role grief plays in creating THRIVING TRANSITIONS. It's important to know exactly what loss you are grieving, and then you can begin to work through the stages of grief.

Since you already identified the loss in the last chapter, let's explore it a little deeper here. There may be multiple losses you feel from one event, so it's important to really FEEL and dive deep into your emotions as you contemplate the loss/losses you are experiencing.

It's also important to note that sometimes when people finally decide to work through a difficult experience it can be years after the initial loss actually happened. If this is the case for you, think back on the months or years since the initial loss and identify all the losses you've already experienced.

The reason? It's important to identify all the reasons why we absolutely must take the Steps to THRIVE. By thinking back on all the things you've already lost, you are actually priming yourself to associate the pain you've experienced in the past to choosing not to change. This helps create the leverage needed to finally make the commitment to thriving.

What are all the smaller things I feel I am losing in relation to the major loss I've experienced? Am I losing security? Am I losing the idea of what I thought my life should look like? Am I losing friendships? Am I losing a feeling of connection or losing my sense of self? What are some of the comforts I am losing? What am I choosing to give up? What have I already lost?

_____

_____

_____

_____

_____

_____

_____

_____

_____

_____

_____

_____

_____

What feelings do I associate with this loss? Am I sad, scared, empty, angry, bitter, lost, bewildered?

_____

_____

_____

_____

_____

_____

_____

_____

*The magic in everything we do to improve ourselves is found in the emotions of our lives. To create a lasting, powerful, and positive transition, we have to get out of our heads and into our hearts. We can't simply distract ourselves from feeling the loss of a loved one and expect that we will create a positive transition. Feelings will always rear their ugly head somewhere down the road when we try to bury them, and unfortunately, they usually end up costing us a lot more the longer we wait to deal with them. As you think about all the feelings you associate with the loss you are experiencing, take your time. Physically and mentally be present with these feelings so that you can effectively move forward to thriving.

Now that you've identified the loss you're experiencing, and the feelings associated, it's important to work through grieving the loss fully. I wish I could tell you there was some kind of magical way to avoid the stages of grief. I wish it was as simple as grieving once and moving on, but life isn't that straight-forward or easy. The stages of grief are hard. Sometimes you need a counselor or coach to help you through. Sometimes you want to talk about the loss over and over until you feel like you've exhausted everyone around you. Sometimes you just need time. (I say this cautiously. Time can help to ease the initial shock, but only if you're also working through the pain in the process. Bottled up grief usually doesn't get better with time.)

In a world of instant everything, it's hard to accept that grieving takes time. It's not a process you can rush. Of course, there are very different levels of grief people experience, and what may cause one person deep anguish could sound like a walk in the park to the next. You have to be your own judge. You have to ask yourself whether or not you are fully experiencing each of the stages of grief as you work through them. No one else can do the work for you, but if you do it, I promise you, it'll be worth it.

STAGES OF GRIEF

Elisabeth Kübler-Ross first proposed the five stages of grief in her 1969 book *On Death and Dying*. Since then, her idea of these stages has become universal for people as they work through grief.

THE FIVE STAGES OF GRIEF:

DENIAL AND ISOLATION
ANGER
BARGAINING
DEPRESSION
ACCEPTANCE

As with our THRIVING THROUGH TRANSITIONS program, the stages of grief are not rigid or structured. You may find yourself in the bargaining stage and then need to go back to the stage of denial. TRUST YOUR OWN PROCESS.

Remember that ultimately, we are all working through the TRANSITION called LIFE. It is full of ups and downs, and twists and turns. BE PATIENT with yourself as you navigate the seas of change. Give yourself time to process each stage as you grieve, and then continue through the Steps of THRIVING THROUGH TRANSITIONS.

DENIAL AND ISOLATION

Often our first instinct when experiencing a loss or choosing to make significant changes is to deny what has happened or is happening: "She can't be gone!", "The x-ray results can't be right!" or "It can't be over!"

Sometimes denial can be much less obvious. It can be an internal conversation that seeks to numb our fears: "It hasn't all been in vain", "This marriage isn't really failing" or "It's not as bad as theirs."

Denial might look like changing majors after several years of college as a way to avoid or defer moving from student life to a career. Sometimes it can be as simple as trying to convince ourselves, "I don't really want it that bad", when it comes to making a career change or starting our own business.

DENIAL ACTS AS A BUFFER for the pain we experience. It's too painful to admit that we have failed at something, or too painful to think that we will never see our loved one again. It's too hard to come to the conclusion that we tried to start a business, and maybe it didn't happen in the time or space that we wanted it to. In many cases, denial eases the blow.

Many times, isolation comes a little later. It can show up when people withdraw from their friends or when they put up walls making sure no one can ever 'hurt them like that again'. Another way it shows up is when someone steps away from the responsibilities of everyday life.

I remember thinking when I found my Dad, "There is no way he could possibly be dead. He's a healthy 43-year-old. That doesn't happen." For months I remember trying to figure out in my head how someone could pass away just like that with no warning signs. I remember obsessing over the cause of his death as if, by some miracle, he'd still be alive if I could just figure it out. It's crazy what our minds can conceive of when we are in the depths of despair.

A few years after my Father's death, my marriage began to fail, but because of denial I kept thinking, "If I just try harder, maybe I can make this work." I couldn't bear to think of the possibility that divorce was going to be a part of my story. That wasn't the plan I had for my life AT ALL! Then, the closer I got to the end, the more isolation set in. I felt completely alone, and I had kept all of my thoughts and feelings from my husband. I remember quite literally feeling like I was married to a complete stranger. And yet, when a marriage counselor told us there was no possibility in her mind that our marriage would make it, I found myself thinking, "I'll show her!" Denial and isolation. They definitely softened the blow for me. I'm sure by the time I finally threw in the towel, an outsider would've thought I moved on really quickly. But I had spent months going through that first step of grief while I was still married.

That's the thing about DENIAL AND ISOLATION. Many times, no one around us knows that we are going through this stage because it's an internal dialogue that we don't express. Probably because we know how crazy it might sound to say it all out loud.

"Hey guys, I know my Dad died, but he was really healthy. I'm thinking if I can just get to the bottom of this and figure out why he died, things might be different," or "I know I've been in a miserable relationship for the past ten years, and my husband has cheated on me at least seven times (that I know of), but I really feel like this time is going to be different. He promised he wouldn't do it anymore. I know he's told me the same thing the past 6 times I've caught him, but he said he wants to work on us."

Clearly those are irrational thoughts, but we tell ourselves those kinds of internal stories all the time (even subconsciously). Denial and isolation create a buffer against the pain we'd experience if we told ourselves the truth.

As you walk through your TRANSITION, you may have already experienced the stage of DENIAL AND ISOLATION. You may not realize you've experienced this stage until AFTER you experience it. It makes sense. NO ONE IN DENIAL THINKS THEY ARE IN DENIAL. In any case, it's important that we take some time to reflect and notice whether we've already worked through this stage of grief, or if we maybe notice some things we are currently in denial about or withdrawn and isolated from. Becoming self-aware is a great place to begin. So, let's get started:

What have I been in denial about in regard to my transition? Am I in denial about how hard it is to make the change? Am I in denial that what I've been doing isn't really working? Am I in denial about a circumstance or event that has been a tragic loss for me? Get as clear and specific as possible.

_____

_____

_____

_____

_____

_____

_____

How have I isolated myself? Have I felt withdrawn? Have I felt a general sense of depression or deadening inside? Have I isolated myself from certain people or circumstances? Do I preoccupy myself so as not to face an aspect of my transition?

_____

_____

_____

_____

_____

_____

_____

Do I have work to do to become more self-aware and confront areas of denial? Do I need to ask for another person's opinion about how I am handling my transition? Can I call on a close loved one to help me see through a different lens? Deep down, do I feel like I am being 100% honest with myself in regard to the transition I am facing?

_____

_____

_____

_____

_____

_____

_____

ANGER

"Holding onto anger is like drinking poison and expecting the other person to die." —Buddha

As denial and isolation act as a buffer for our pain, we quickly realize that by working through them, we open ourselves to the REALITY of our situation... And that can be VERY PAINFUL. In our vulnerability we often MASK OUR PAIN AS ANGER.

It can be too hard and painful to accept the transition we face, so instead we become angry. We become angry at the doctor who diagnosed the cancer. We become angry at the spouse who cheated, even though we saw the marriage failing for months prior. We become angry that we got fired despite hating the job in the first place.

Why? Because ANGER IS SAFE. Anger places blame on someone or something else, and it takes our mind off of the real problem—THAT CHANGE CAN BE EXTREMELY PAINFUL.

WHENEVER WE
MOVE THROUGH
A *Transition* WE
ARE MOVING AWAY
FROM ONE THING
AND TOWARD
ANOTHER, AND
THAT USUALLY
COMES WITH THE
PAIN OF LOSS.

IN OUR *vulnerability* WE OFTEN MASK OUR PAIN AS ANGER.

As you work through the stages of grief, Anger is okay! We all experience feeling angry at times. We just have to be sure to WORK THROUGH THE ANGER WE FEEL, so it doesn't control us. We have to be certain that we let go of the anger before it poisons us.

How do we do that? First, by RECOGNIZING THE ANGER. Second, by IDENTIFYING THE PAIN we are trying to mask.

Take this example from my own life:

My marriage had been failing since day one. I was nineteen and chose to marry someone twenty-three years my senior. I was pregnant and scared, and marriage seemed like the obvious choice to bring me the sense of security and connectedness my life was missing. Unfortunately, you can't build a solid foundation rushing into marriage needy and insecure.

Obviously, I was broken and so was my now ex-husband. So, as you can imagine, our marriage was built like a house of cards. Our foundation was flimsy and weak. It was constructed out of fear and a need to feel in control of the situation.

Deep in my soul, I knew our marriage was all wrong. I knew this wasn't even close to the plan I had for my life, but I was scared. Duping my marriage, I lived in DENIAL. I kept trying to do more for my marriage and have a better attitude toward my husband, but then, ANGER set in. I blamed him for everything that was wrong in my life. I blamed him for taking advantage of my youth and naivety. I blamed him for treating me poorly.

And then, I started becoming ANGRY with MYSELF. How could I have strayed so far off my plan for my life? How could I have been so stupid to get pregnant and married at nineteen? How could I not see how mean he was to me? What was wrong with me? Why didn't I value myself? And now that I had children to think about, how could I be so selfish to even consider divorce and disrupting their lives?

I was drinking that poison and a lot of it. I felt myself becoming a monster. I felt myself hating life and becoming angrier and angrier, until finally, one day, the band-aid was ripped off and all the pain that was boiling inside of me finally exploded. I WAS DONE. I was done feeling angry. I was done feeling alone. I was done with all of it. And that day was a PAINFUL one! There were no more excuses, no more reasons to be angry. It was over, and it finally didn't matter to me why. I was able to finally get past my ANGER and onto the next stage of grief.

This is just one small example of how quickly anger can become toxic. I can think of countless other times throughout my varied transitions where I dealt with anger on many levels.

Sometimes the anger we experience is obvious, but other times it's subtle. Sometimes our anger has no voice and other times it can be blaring. Anger looks different for each person, but the result is the same–over time anger becomes an insidious poison that can consume us if we aren't careful.

Let's identify the ANGER you've felt or currently feel regarding your own transition:

Who or what is the target of your ANGER? Is it a boss, a spouse, a situation? Do you feel ANGER towards yourself? Do you feel wronged or punished? Is your anger even deeper? Maybe you feel angry toward God or the Universe?

_____

_____

_____

_____

_____

_____

_____

_____

_____

_____

What PAIN are you masking? Is it a feeling of INADEQUACY? Is it FEAR? Is it UNCERTAINTY? Do you feel ALONE? Are you masking the pain of REGRET? Are you angry because something is UNFAIR?

_____

_____

_____

_____

_____

What beliefs keep you in your anger? How do you justify the anger? How is your anger serving you?

_____

_____

_____

_____

_____

_____

_____

_____

BARGAINING

Often as we process our grief, BARGAINING and ANGER can come almost simultaneously. At one moment we may feel anger, and at the next, we are making a deal with ourselves or our higher power, "If you could just cure the cancer, I'll be a better person," or "If I just try harder at loving my husband, he won't cheat on me anymore."

BARGAINING IS OUR ATTEMPT TO CONTROL THE SITUATION. It is our way of feeling in control in the midst of our pain. We start to analyze anything and everything that is within our power.

In my example, I began bargaining with myself by thinking, "If I just show my husband more love, or show him what a good wife I am, our marriage will be better."

Unfortunately, we can't always BARGAIN ourselves into the outcome we desire. We can't have our cancer cured by promising to be a better person. We can't control our spouse or make them stop cheating. We can't bring a loved one back from the dead

BARGAINING IS OUR ATTEMPT TO *control* THE SITUATION.

by thinking about what we would have done differently. We can't stop a layoff by begging and pleading with our boss not to fire us.

There are circumstances where it is wise to exhaust all possible resources, but that isn't the same as BARGAINING. If your marriage is important to you, talk to your spouse (and listen), pray, try counseling, read books, attend classes. Take actions to improve yourself and understand your spouse before calling it quits. If you're faced with cancer, definitely research all your treatment options and get multiple expert opinions. Bargaining is different. BARGAINING IS TRYING TO CONTROL OUR SITUATION WHEN THE SITUATION IS OUT OF OUR CONTROL.

What agreements or BARGAINS have I made?

_____

_____

_____

_____

_____

_____

What about my transition am I ATTEMPTING TO CONTROL with that bargaining?

_____

_____

_____

_____

_____

Am I in DENIAL about the reality of my transition and using BARGAINING TECHNIQUES to mask my ANGER?

_____

_____

_____

_____

_____

What would happen if I let go of my attempts to control everything? If I surrendered to WHAT IS?

_____

_____

_____

_____

_____

_____

_____

_____

_____

DEPRESSION

As we continue to move through the process of grief, DEPRESSION IS WHEN WE BEGIN TO EXPERIENCE GRIEF ON A DEEPER LEVEL. We often times go through a period of emptiness or deep sadness while mourning what once was.

You may start to wonder, "What's the point of all this anyway?" You may find it hard to get out of bed in the morning. This is generally when apathy and a sense of doom can set in.

I remember this phase well after my Dad's passing. I remember the feeling that I just couldn't get back to living life. This pain was especially strong in the months after his funeral when everyone else went back to "normal" while I sat back feeling paralyzed and not knowing how to live again. Every morning when I'd wake up I knew I needed to take care of my kids, but there was no joy, no excitement, and I was living life in the dim colorless state that is depression. I knew I didn't want to feel this way, but I didn't see any way out of it.

Realizing I needed the help of a professional was my saving grace. Sometimes, as I'll share later on, we have to help ourselves through this stage by asking for others to hold us accountable and push us to re-engage with life.

It's important to realize that DEPRESSION AS A STAGE OF GRIEF IS NOT THE SAME AS CLINICAL DEPRESSION–IT'S A NATURAL RESPONSE TO LOSS. It is not only necessary, but important to work through the emotions you feel as you transition from one way of life to a different one.

As Kübler-Ross puts it, "Make a place for your guest. Invite your depression to pull up a chair with you in front of the fire, and sit with it, without looking for a way to escape. Allow the sadness and emptiness to cleanse you and help you explore your loss in its entirety."

When it comes to working through our TRANSITION, not every person will experience the same level of GRIEF, so you may find that DEPRESSION isn't part of your TRANSITION process. Often, however, depression is very much a part of our grieving process, especially when working through some of the difficult transitions we've talked about.

In these cases, you will experience times of SADNESS, LONELINESS and LOSS. It's critical that you make sure to ALLOW YOURSELF TO FEEL THE EMOTIONS AS THEY ARISE. Spend some time in solitude and dive deep into your sadness and loss. Really feel the sadness. Feel the emptiness. Have a good long cry. Scream if you need to. Feel the emotions that you need to feel as hard as it may be.

ACCEPTANCE

The final stage of our grieving process is ACCEPTANCE. DEPRESSION finally moves us forward into acceptance of our *new reality*. Some days we can accept our new reality easily and effortlessly, while other days it is a struggle.

Acceptance doesn't mean the struggle is over, it simply means you are ready to MOVE FORWARD. It doesn't mean the bad days are forever behind you. It simply means that you are ready and open to experiencing brighter days. You may find yourself continually having to come back to a place of acceptance, especially if the loss you've suffered has been exceptionally difficult.

Remember, just like the other Steps, you may have to experience the stages of grief multiple times before you're ready to move forward. The key is to REALLY EXPERIENCE them, and to ALLOW YOURSELF TIME TO HEAL.

Have I accepted the reality of my current situation? Explain.

_____

_____

_____

_____

_____

_____

_____

What does my new reality look like?

_____

_____

_____

_____

_____

_____

_____

What are some examples that show at least the beginning of my acceptance (where previously in this process I would have demonstrated denial/isolation/ anger/depression)?

_____

_____

_____

_____

_____

_____

_____

_____

How do I feel about accepting this reality? Am I scared, sad, hopeful, peaceful?

_____

_____

_____

_____

_____

_____

_____

_____

Do I feel ready to move forward into the next step of my transition? How will I manage (or even leverage) the feelings I expressed above as I move forward? Do I have any ideas or expectations or fears about what moving forward looks like?

_____

_____

_____

_____

_____

_____

_____

_____

_____

_____

_____

_____

_____

_____

_____

_____

_____

_____

_____

STEP 2

Reframe.

IN ORDER TO GET BACK INTO LIVING FULLY, WE MUST OPEN OURSELVES UP TO THE *possibility* THAT WE CAN CHOOSE TO BENEFIT FROM EVEN THE WORST SITUATIONS.

STEP 2 - REFRAME.
REFRAME THE EXPERIENCE

"The primary cause of unhappiness is never the situation, but your thoughts about it." —Eckhart Tolle

Now that we've grieved our loss, it's time to take our transition and benefit from it. Now, you may be thinking I'm crazy, or you could possibly have some anger rising up at my even suggesting that you benefit from your pain and loss, but hopefully by now, there is a sense of trust. Hopefully, you can feel that I'm just another soul on her own transitional journey who truly wants to help people as they experience their own challenges and pain.

I know first-hand how difficult this next step can be to work through, but in order to get back into living fully, we must open ourselves up to the possibility that we can choose to benefit from even the worst situations. REFRAMING THE EXPERIENCE is all about reprogramming the framework of our existing assumptions, beliefs, and values. It's about rewriting our scripts to EMPOWER us to move forward and experience the happiness and joy that comes from journeying to our Point B.

In order to do this successfully, we first have to recognize the lens/lenses through which we currently view the world. We each have an extensive set of values and beliefs. Usually they are formed as the result of our biology and our experiences as a young person. We had people, such as our parents, teachers, and friends, who helped shape our perspectives—sometimes for the better, sometimes for the worse.

As we grow into adulthood, sometimes we start to question those values and beliefs. Often our experiences (the transitional phases of our lives) spontaneously reshape what we previously thought to be the truth, the whole truth, and nothing but the truth. I was (in retrospect) fortunate enough to grow up in a house where beliefs and ideas were ever-changing.

**(Full disclaimer before I share this story: I talk about my personal experiences with different religions. In no way do I think poorly of any of the religions I speak about, and my personal belief is that LOVE is the answer to all, so please know before reading that my intention is only to share my experience in the hopes that it highlights the way we all frame and reframe our views of the world as we experience life.)

My Father was a seeker. He had a difficult time wrestling with his childhood, some of his experiences as a young adult, and his need for love and acceptance. We changed religions quite often as a result. Looking back, I think he deeply yearned for love and acceptance, but didn't realize he needed to start with loving himself. For most of my early adolescent years we attended a Mormon Church. I was even baptized there at age 8. By the time I hit my tween years though, we had left the church—partially because of my Dad's desire for change, and partially because of my own need to feel safe after being molested.

I started attending a Christian Youth Group at a local church that many of my friends belonged to, and while I enjoyed the social aspect of it, I never really felt a personal connection to God there. Inevitably, someone would find out I grew up Mormon and the judgement would start. I hated that part of my experience. I felt like church was the one place where people were supposed to be kind, generous and loving, but I found many people to be quite the opposite.

At home, my Dad's teasing was relentless. Why anyone would go to one of those 'holy roller' places was beyond anything my Dad could comprehend. Needless to say, I attended off and on throughout high school, never getting too "into it" in an effort to keep the teasing to a minimum.

When I was a junior in high school, I had the chance to attend a private Catholic school. The two years I spent there were some of the fondest memories of my life. I really discovered myself there. Still, I didn't find a deep connection to the Catholic religion, but I led several retreats and definitely felt the presence of God working in my life.

Later on, my Dad experimented with some of the Eastern Religions and I was introduced to meditation. Once again, my Dad didn't really stick to his new-found enlightenment, but I was fortunate enough to have been exposed to these new ideas. As a young adult, I wasn't really interested in learning to become more peaceful or connected, but I found my way back to the amazing power of meditation later on.

Today, after being introduced to so many different ideas, religions, and philosophies, I've discovered what makes me personally connected to God, the Universe, my Higher Power. For me, I feel most connected while in nature. I still enjoy a good Sunday service from time to time and pray and meditate often, but nature is the place where I feel peace, connection, and Divine love from my Creator.

What does all this have to do with REFRAMING YOUR EXPERIENCE? I was blessed from a young age to look at experiences as opportunities to GROW and CHANGE because of my Dad's journey. I'm grateful for the framework it created for me because it gave me the tools to question things for myself—to continually decide whether ideas I've been exposed to fit within my world-view.

Adaptability is one of the greatest strengths we can possess, and there is no better way to cultivate it than to consciously transition from one idea to another. Whether your transition is physical, mental, or emotional, REFRAMING is about reworking our beliefs and values to align with our experiences.

There is no sense in holding onto a belief that when someone dies, that's it—lights out, game over, if that belief no longer serves you. Maybe you close yourself off to the opportunity to connect to your loved one who's passed on because your belief system is holding you back.

Or maybe you have a belief that says, "My ex-husband was a cheater, so I'll never trust another man again. They're all cheaters." How useful is that in creating a thriving transition?

Perhaps your belief is that, since you lost your last job, you'll never succeed at anything. You're a loser, and even if you get hired somewhere, chances are they'll probably fire you too.

Again, please know that my intention isn't to change your beliefs, but only to help you look at them for yourself and examine whether or not they help and empower you. Most of the time, our beliefs fall into one of two categories, and it's important to identify where most of your beliefs lie.

The first category is *Fixed Beliefs*. Fixed Beliefs are easy to identify because they tend to follow a cause and effect pattern. For instance:

Life happens to me.
I'm just unlucky.
Why try?
There is nothing I can do to change anything.
It's someone/something else's fault.
My happiness is the result of my circumstances.

The other category of beliefs is *Growth Beliefs*. Growth Beliefs are more empowering and tend to focus on possibilities rather than problems. A Growth Mindset believes that:

I am the creator of my own reality.
I choose the way I feel regardless of my circumstances.
Life is good despite setbacks and obstacles.
I am responsible for the quality of my life.
I will keep trying regardless of setbacks.

My guess is that if you are reading this, your belief system is more in-tune with the latter. Typically, people with a fixed mindset aren't going to be doing a lot of reading to improve their lives because, "life just happens to them", right?

So, I want to congratulate you! There aren't a lot of people in this world who recognize their power to create and reframe their beliefs, and the world definitely needs more of us!

You might be thinking, "I've always been a pretty positive person. I've taken responsibility for my life, but this transition has rocked me to my core, and I don't feel very hopeful right now."

That's OK! I think we all go through self-doubt and questioning during our toughest

Reframing YOUR EXPERIENCE IS ALL ABOUT FINDING THOSE HEROIC QUALITIES OF YOUR STORY.

moments. As I approached the transition to life-coach, I nearly succumbed to pressure from people who loved me, who didn't want to see me get hurt, who believed starting a coaching business was just too much to take on with three kids and an already profitable business as a stylist. I've felt like giving up at times myself, so I understand where they are coming from, but comfort and security isn't going to get me to where I want to go in life. We all experience setbacks. We all fear failure. Even the most positive person struggles from time to time.

The important thing to take note of is that—if you've read this far—you have already recognized your desire to THRIVE through your tough spot, even if you have no clue how you're going to do it yet.

Reframing our stories really has a lot to do with our perception of negative events in our lives. Most of the time we frame loss with a very negative set of lenses, but if we think about most of the success stories of our time, they all have something in common. The stories were, at some point, rooted in pain.

Elizabeth Gilbert said it best, "We all want things to stay the same. Settle for living in misery because we are afraid of change, of things crumbling to ruins. Ruin is a gift. Ruin is the road to transformation."

Isn't that a great way to frame our painful experiences? As if the darkest days of our lives are really the greatest blessings of all?

Recently, at the Tony Robbins seminar I attended, he challenged all of us to take this idea of REFRAMING even further to embrace the idea that, *"Life does not happen TO you, it happens FOR you."* Probably not what you want to hear after losing a loved one or failing at something you poured your heart and soul into. But what if it's true? What if everything we've experienced in this life, the good and the bad, are all really, truly happening FOR us?

This isn't a new idea. We see this theme a lot in literature. "The Hero's Journey" is a pattern of narrative story-telling in which Joseph Campbell, an American writer who focused most of his works around the human experience, describes 17 steps the hero of any story goes through.

It's been further refined into three major categories:

Departure
Initiation
Return

If you look at any Disney film, you will see this template. Campbell and other scholars have also described the lives of some of the most influential leaders our world has ever known in terms of "The Hero's Journey". The lives of people like Buddha and Jesus Christ fit the narrative quite well.

You might be thinking by now, "This is all great, but I didn't purchase this course on transitions to learn about narratives and story-telling." Humor me.

As I learned more about "The Hero's Journey" I became intrigued with one particular piece of the journey. As I navigated my own transition, this piece gave me great hope and excitement for my future. It was the reason I was able to REFRAME MY EXPERIENCE. It made me feel like I was being granted access to this private, exclusive club that only The Greats were invited to.

What was this secret piece of the puzzle I'd been missing? It was the part of the journey, during the initiation phase, where the hero is presented with some major obstacle he has to overcome. It's so obvious, but I had never thought about it before; there would be no hero in any story without having to endure trials and challenges—without having to face transition.

This is an exciting realization for people like you and me who are navigating major transitions in our lives. REFRAMING YOUR EXPERIENCE is all about finding those heroic qualities of your story. It's about coming to the realization that perhaps you are meant for something far greater than you previously could've imagined. It's about seeing the positive aspects of going through this transition.

A few years back I went with my family to watch the movie *Unbroken,* based on the book by the same title. If you aren't familiar with it, it's the story of a man named Louis "Louie" Zamperini who, as a young boy was always getting into trouble. Later in life, he endured things that most people would consider humanly impossible. While in the military during WWII, he spent 47 days in a life raft after his plane crashed in the middle of the Pacific Ocean only to be rescued by the Japanese navy who proceeded to torture him as a prisoner for two years before his rescue.

How did he survive? As the movie depicts, Louie was a man who was unbreakable. Suddenly, his stubbornness as a child had a purpose! That strong will enabled him to live through what would cause most people to crumble. That's what reframing is all about. It's about finding whatever that little sliver of good is. I'm sure as hard as it was to raise a child as obstinate as Louie, his family felt immense gratitude knowing that same tough spirit enabled him to survive against all odds.

You may not feel like the hero Louie was. You may not feel like a hero for simply choosing to end a toxic relationship, or for choosing to thrive through the death of someone you love, but YOU ARE. You are the HERO OF YOUR OWN STORY and you may very well be a hero to others also! Sometimes we don't even realize how many other people we inspire in the process of navigating our transitions.

I can't tell you how many people have come to me in the past ten years and told me how I inspired them because of the way I handled my Dad's death. I've also had the opportunity to be there for people I love during their own painful experiences only because I knew the pain they were going through.

Shortly after meeting the man who is now my husband, his Mom suffered a terrible stroke and was given only a few days to live. Unfortunately, the stroke was a side effect of cancer that had metastasized throughout her body. At this point there was nothing more they could do. While we had only been dating for three short weeks, he turned to me for support and understanding. I found myself deeply involved in his experience because I understood the grief he was going through. (I understood that on his worst days he was missing his mom, and I was able to detach myself from feeling responsible for his experience.) Losing my Dad became this great gift of understanding him in those moments.

That's just one example of REFRAMING. It's about looking at the situation and finding all the possible seeds of good that can come out of it, no matter how impossible that may seem.

The good I found in living through a bad marriage is another instance of REFRAMING in my life. I never would've fully appreciated certain qualities about my current husband if I hadn't suffered the pain of my first marriage. I had no idea that a man could be so loving and kind-hearted to me, but I can almost guarantee that I would have taken that for granted without the experience of my first marriage. I also know I would have been more judgmental of others' relationships. I wouldn't have fully understood the pain a parent feels when they don't see their child for an extended period of time. I probably also wouldn't have learned from all the things that I did wrong in my marriage–talking poorly about my spouse, cowering to his mood swings, and feeling responsible for all of his feelings.

As you go through the process of REFRAMING YOUR EXPERIENCE, the goal is to feel immense gratitude and joy for the transition you are going through. Find every silver-lining you can. Try to make your glass overflow with positivity. If there is a seed for something good to come out of your situation–find it.

Maybe you'll decide to use your own experiences to help others. Maybe you'll find the loving partner you deserve. Maybe you'll decide to start a business you've always thought about starting, but never would have stepped into fully because of the security you felt at your job. Whatever the case may be, there is ALWAYS a seed for something great to come out of a seemingly negative situation.

"Some changes look negative on the surface, but you will soon realize that space is being created in your life for something new to emerge."
–Eckhart Tolle

Which of my personal beliefs have been challenged as a result of this transition?

_____

_____

_____

_____

_____

_____

What perspectives are holding me back?

_____

_____

_____

_____

_____

_____

What lessons have I learned? What will I do differently now?

_____

_____

_____

_____

_____

_____

How have I changed and grown because of this experience? Has my understanding deepened in some areas? What do I know about myself that I didn't know before? How will that information affect how I move forward?

_____

_____

_____

_____

What are all the "positive seeds" of this experience? In other words, what are all the possible positive outcomes of this transition?

_____

_____

_____

_____

_____

_____

_____

_____

How will this transition affect other areas of my life? In what positive ways could other areas of my life shift as a result of this transition?

_____

_____

_____

_____

_____

_____

_____

_____

_____

In what ways have my beliefs, perspectives, and values changed because of this experience?

_____

_____

_____

_____

_____

_____

_____

_____

Could I possibly mitigate any of the negative feelings I have regarding my transition? If so, how?

_____

_____

_____

_____

_____

_____

_____

_____

_____

_____

What am I most grateful for regarding this transition? Why? Try to think in terms of feelings because our power to change subconsciously is attached to our feelings.

"Change the way you look at things and the things you look at change." –Wayne W. Dyer

Now that you've answered these tough questions the goal is to keep the positive aspects alive and in the forefront of your mind. Because our subconscious mind is guided not by thoughts, but by feelings, the goal is to get into a state of feeling positive about your transition as much as possible.

There are so many wonderful techniques for creating the positive feelings needed to create subconscious change. You could daydream about all the new, exciting possibilities this transition is bringing you. You could write in a gratitude journal each day about all the reasons you are thankful for your transition. You could go on a walk each morning with the intention of building yourself up by congratulating yourself on your strength, resolve, and determination as you go through your transition. It really doesn't matter which tactic you use, as long as it helps you stir a positive, emotional connection to your transition.

As we continue through the program, you'll discover even more ways to get into a positive state. Sometimes we have a hard time REFRAMING OUR TRANSITION because we don't really know what we're moving towards, or we don't want to move in a new direction. Sometimes we are so focused on the past and dwelling on the pain of moving away from something or someone we loved, that we aren't even living. If that's the case for you, the next step should help.

STEP 3

Center.

GETTING *centered* IN THE PRESENT IS ONE OF THE FASTEST WAYS TO CHANGE OUR WHOLE OUTLOOK ON LIFE.

STEP 3 - CENTER.
GET CENTERED IN THE PRESENT

"There are only two days in the year that nothing can be done. One is called yesterday and the other is called tomorrow, so today is the right day to love, believe, do and mostly to live." —Dalai Lama

If I could recommend only one chapter of this book, this would be it. Getting centered in the present is one of the fastest ways to change our whole outlook on life. It brings peace and helps us LIVE OUR BEST LIFE. Most of us are so busy and so used to keeping ourselves busy that we don't take much time to really GET CENTERED IN THE PRESENT.

I remember during my divorce I had times where I would start spinning. I felt like my whole life was out of control. I would worry and OBSESS about how I would pay the bills next month or if my kids were going to be ok. I felt this never ceasing chatter in my head.

"Will anyone ever love me? Am I going to be able to make it on my own? Are my kids going to hate me? Am I strong enough? What if I can't make enough money to support my kids?"

I think many of us have similar reels playing over and over in our heads. We worry about our loved ones. We worry about being accepted by our peers. We worry about our finances. We worry about being loved. We worry about the things we cannot change, like the death of a loved one. Unfortunately, all this does is put us in a place where we manifest our fears, and IT ROBS US OF THE OPPORTUNITY FOR JOY IN THE PRESENT.

I learned firsthand how worrying steals from our lives. I've lost many years to the life-sucking habit of worrying. Prior to my Dad's death, I experienced another difficult transition. This transition was the type that totally robbed me of joy in the present.

Growing up I had a wonderful family. I'm the oldest of 5 kids and my Parents were very loving and involved. My Mom was always the room parent in our classes, and my Dad was the coach. He coached me early on in t-ball, and then continued coaching my brothers in their various sports as we got older. Our house was always the place kids wanted to be because my Parents created such a warm environment and it was important to them that people felt welcome and had fun.

So, you'll understand why I was in complete and utter shock to discover shortly after high school that my Dad had been living a double life. Unbeknownst to my Mom or us kids, he had been doing some very shady business and it finally caught up with him. He was indicted on October 19, 2006 for money laundering and fraud. If that wasn't enough, we also learned that he'd been having an affair for several years with a stripper, which ended my parent's marriage 6 months shy of what would have been their 20th anniversary. My life was completely flipped upside down.

Over the course of the next year, I found out that somehow my identity had been used for some of my Dad's dealings and because of that I was forced to talk to federal prosecutors. While I knew I hadn't done anything wrong, there was nothing more intimidating than pulling into my driveway to be greeted by six federal agents wanting to know everything they could about my Dad's secret life.

I can honestly say that I lost that year of my life to worrying about everything that had to do with his case. I stressed about how it would affect my younger siblings. I ruminated about whether or not my Dad would go to jail and if he did go, how long would it be for? I worried about how my Mom was going to make it through all the pain and uncertainty she was experiencing. I thought and thought about how angry and upset I was that my Dad did this to our family.

In the end, my Dad was sentenced to five years in Federal Prison on August 21, 2007. He was given two months to handle his affairs before turning himself in. And then… guess what?

He died the weekend before he was supposed to turn himself in. And I realized in a single moment how stupid it was to spend all that time worrying and being upset about something that never even materialized. Suddenly, I went from worrying about how we'd get through the five years in prison to something I hadn't considered or worried about at all-how we'd get through the rest of our lives without our Dad who, despite the terrible things he'd done, was still someone who loved us deeply and wanted to make things right.

Since then, I've rediscovered the great gift and blessing of living life more mindfully. Sure, I still worry at times, but now I am quicker to recognize the patterns that lead me to worry. I've also learned some wonderful techniques to help me get back to being CENTERED in the present moment.

Some of the techniques I've found most helpful—both in my personal life and in the lives of the people I've worked with—are breathing exercises, meditation, expressing gratitude, exploring nature, giving to others, and exercise. These techniques all share a common thread of calming the mind and refocusing a person's energy on what is happening right there in the moment.

What I'd like you to do is choose the methods that speak to you, and don't worry about the ones that don't. I've always believed that to really know what works best for us, we have to give things a try. I recommend exploring some, or all, of these to see what really feels best for you. I've compiled several resources to guide you through each option. As with all the Steps, give yourself plenty of time to really work through GETTING CENTERED IN THE PRESENT. You will experience greater healing and will be able to successfully navigate your transition by allowing yourself to go at your own pace. You might feel the urge to rush through, but don't give in. Be patient and gentle with yourself!

Remember that results don't happen overnight. I've talked to many people who say they've tried meditation and it didn't work for them, and then after talking more, I find out that they tried it one time. Of course, it didn't work! You can't eat one healthy meal and expect to instantly get skinny or go on one run and be fit for life. So, if you're someone who routinely experiences anxiety, stress, or worry, don't expect that you'll feel the effects of any of these techniques right away. Commit to consistently applying one or two of these techniques for at least 30 days before you decide whether they work for you.

I've also included a free resource at www.thrivingthroughtransitions.com to document your progress while trying any of these techniques. I personally enjoy documenting my growth because I love looking back and realizing how far I've come and how different my life is as a result. When we get to Step 5 – Take Action, we'll also go more in depth on creating an action plan specifically for you.

BREATHING EXERCISES

"To control the breathing is to control the mind. With different patterns of breathing, you can fall in love, you can hate someone, you can feel the whole spectrum of feelings just by changing your breathing."
–Marina Abramovic

One of the fastest ways to change our physiology and GET CENTERED is through breathing exercises. When we are scared, overwhelmed, upset, experiencing pain, or feeling rejection, our breath often becomes shallow and tense. Simply taking a few deep breaths can dramatically change our physiology in a matter of seconds.

Science is now acknowledging what ancient yogis have known forever. Using breath control, or pranayama, we can slow down our nervous system, reduce symptoms of anxiety and depression, and even help cure post-traumatic stress disorder.

The ways breathing exercises can help us are truly astounding. However, most of us only experience breath as it happens automatically–without the added benefits to health and happiness.

Let's try a simple experiment. I want you to notice your breath. Is it shallow or deep? Is it swift or slow? Is it forceful or soft? Without changing anything else, I'd like you to breathe in through your nose for four counts and then out through your nose for four counts. Repeat the process 10 times (or go for five minutes for even better results).

How do you feel? Although basic, most people experience a greater sense of peace and calm after utilizing this equal breathing method, also called Sama Vritti. Once you get the basic pranayama (breathing technique) down, try to increase the breaths from 4 seconds to 6 or 8 seconds.

Breathing exercises are so beneficial that I've put together a quick-reference chart with some of the best breathing methods and when to use them. You'll find this chart along with many other free resources at www.thrivingthroughtransitions.com.

MEDITATION

"Meditation can help us embrace our worries, our fears, our anger; and that is very healing. We let our own natural capacity of healing do the work."
—Thich Nhat Hanh

Meditation is one of the most transformative ways to CENTER yourself. Regular practice can dramatically improve concentration, increase happiness and acceptance, and even slow aging. Meditation takes breathing practices to an even deeper level by controlling thoughts and harnessing our ability to actively be in the present moment.

There are many schools of thought on meditation. Some masters teach meditation within the constraints of stillness while other teachers focus on centering with light movements through yoga or qi gong.

There are also different thoughts on the best practices for getting started. While some experts advise to train with a professional instructor, I would recommend getting your feet wet first if you've never tried anything like this before. I know if I had waited until I had the money and resources to hire a professional I probably still wouldn't be meditating regularly, so my suggestion would be to just start trying different techniques. You'll find what works for you and then, once you start noticing some of the benefits, you can decide if you want to hire a professional instructor who can help you master your practice.

Again, I've put together a simple chart outlining some of my favorite techniques and practices, which you'll find in the resources section over on the website, www. thrivingthroughtransitions.com. This is designed to help you discover which practices you might enjoy and learn some of the wonderful benefits of meditation.
If you are ready to go deeper with meditation, I've found that the Chopra Center and Mind Valley both have a wealth of knowledge and resources on the subject, so I highly recommend popping over to www.chopra.com or www.mindvalleyacademy.com and spending some time exploring.

I USED TO THINK THAT EXPERIENCES DICTATE GRATITUDE, BUT I FULLY BELIEVE NOW THAT *gratitude* CAN DICTATE WHAT WE EXPERIENCE.

Another great resource that is absolutely free is YouTube. Many mornings I choose to do a guided meditation and I've found some great guided meditations there. Meditation can seem hard to a beginner, and at times, you may even question whether you are even doing it at all. This is totally normal and expected. Start small and increase the amount of time you spend meditating gradually. When I began, I could only do five minutes. I started getting stir crazy after that. Now, I can easily do thirty to forty-five-minute meditations and really enjoy the process. However, I know I would have given up if I felt like I had to do a lengthy meditation in the beginning.

GRATITUDE

I can think of nothing that has had a more positive effect on my life than learning to FEEL grateful. I used to think that experiences dictate gratitude, but I fully believe now that gratitude can dictate what we experience. We always get to choose how we respond to the events in our lives, and choosing to feel grateful is one of the most powerful ways to instantly feel better about any situation we face.

One of my favorite books on this subject—a book that has had a profound impact on my life—is a book called *The Magic*. If you struggle with a pessimistic attitude or always feel stressed and full of anxiety, please buy this book. In it, Rhonda Byrne, takes readers through 28 days of gratitude practices and promises readers that if they do the work for 28 days they will experience the 'Magic'.

I can say, based on my own personal experience, that she definitely keeps her promise. The first time I read this book was during one of the most stressful times of my life. We were barely making ends meet. My husband and I had just been married, and he was unexpectedly laid off. Stressed doesn't begin to cover what I was feeling.

I had heard about *The Magic* after being exposed to the film *The Secret*, also by Rhonda Byrne. I was desperate to try anything to make my life less stressful. I committed to faithfully following the steps Byrne outlined in the book, and it completely changed my life! Not only did I manifest material things (a brand-new car, financial security, debt repayment), but I also experienced a level of peace I had never previously experienced in my life. I healed relationships. I felt grateful for all of the 'mistakes' I'd made—the times I used to beat myself up for—I was able to feel deep gratitude for. I truly experienced magic working in my life.

Now, whenever I start to feel stressed or upset with something in my life I know I can instantly refocus my energy on gratitude and once again feel peaceful and blessed.

I've put together a great resource with many ideas for expressing gratitude at www. thrivingthroughtransitions.com, so if you're looking to start building a gratitude practice I'd highly recommend checking it out.

EXPLORING NATURE

"In the presence of nature, a wild delight runs through the man, in spite of real sorrows." —Ralph Waldo Emerson

Sometimes just the simple act of getting out into the world and seeing and experiencing nature can be a great way to GET CENTERED in the present. I enjoy hiking for this reason, and I know countless others who do as well. Whether it's the fresh, clean air we breathe or the overall beauty, there is something amazingly refreshing about getting outside.

If you struggle with meditation, simply going for a walk outside can be an effective alternative. Some people need to move to relax, so if this seems more tolerable to you, schedule some time to just get outside and take it all in.

You can also try to implement breathing techniques while outside for added benefit. Awhile back I went to an Ayurvedic Doctor who instructed me to go on a fifteen-minute walk using what he called, "Darth Vader" breathing. Basically, when you inhale you try to inhale deeply and slowly through your nose and into your throat until you make a sound much like Darth Vader breathing through his mask. It was an analogy that worked well for me. I noticed after my walking sessions I always felt more energized, focused and achieved a sense of internal calm. I still utilize this method of getting centered fairly often because it's so beneficial for me.

GIVE TO OTHERS

"For it is in giving that we receive." —St. Francis of Assisi

Let me tell you a quick little story about giving to others. It was shared with me at a very difficult time in my life, shortly after losing my Dad. I went into work one day, about a month after he passed, and for some reason, was having a particularly hard day. My client had just sat down in my chair (I was a hairstylist) and I started to lose it. I shared with her about my Dad's passing, and then she shared with me that her son had died forty years prior. He had drowned in the bathtub at age three.

It definitely put my pain in perspective. I had two beautiful, healthy boys, so I empathized with the incredible loss she must have felt, and I definitely wasn't prepared for what she said next. To this day, I think this has probably been the best advice I've ever received.

She said, "You know, I don't have any words that can take away the pain you're feeling right now, but I'll share with you a piece of advice I was given by another mother who lost her son…

On your very worst days, the days that seem hopeless, go do something kind for someone. You can do it in your father's honor. You can add to his legacy. I've had some pretty bad days, but you know, you can't be sad when you are giving to others, so I've learned to get out of my head and into my heart on those extra bad days."

That one piece of advice changed my life forever. Fortunately, she was someone I respected and admired, so I was eager to try out her method. And, you know what? It worked! I have used this tactic for dealing with my grief over and over again since then, and I've encouraged others to do the same.

One of my proudest moments was shortly after this conversation. I'd heard about a teenage girl in our community who was battling leukemia. My Dad had a great love for kids, so I knew I wanted to do something to help and act on the advice I was given. I decided to plan a big fundraiser at the salon where I was working. Her Mom had taken time off work to be with her in the hospital, so I figured money would be a huge help to their family.

As the event approached and I got to know the family a little better, I found out that the girl's biggest wish was to be able to get their house remodeled. I felt there couldn't have been a more deserving family to receive something amazing like that, but I was just a twenty-two-year-old hairstylist. I didn't know how I would pull it off, but I knew with my desire to honor my Dad, I would figure it out somehow.

Fortunately, when I want something bad enough, I can be pretty resourceful. I was able to find another woman who partnered with me to start a non-profit organization called *Oregon Dream Makeover*. Within a few short months we lined up some of the most incredible, generous contractors and volunteers and totally remodeled the family's home! It was by far the most transformative experience of my life.

I'm not suggesting that you do something as time consuming as creating a non-profit (although it's a worthy goal if it is something you want to do), but even a small gesture of kindness can significantly change the way you feel and help you become more centered in the present. Maybe try something as simple as buying a stranger's coffee or gas. You could sign up to volunteer for a cause that's important to you. You could look for resources for families that are in need in your local community and see how you could start doing something to help them. You could even decide to join a mission trip to a developing country. Sometimes we need to just get the focus off of ourselves for a minute. It's amazing what giving to others will do. One of the reasons it works so well is that it gets us out of our heads and into our hearts.

EXERCISE

"It is exercise alone that supports the spirits and keeps the mind in vigor."
—Cicero

On a completely different level, exercise is another powerful tool for getting centered. Exercise releases mood-enhancing hormones almost immediately, so it can definitely lift our spirits, but it can also push us to our physical limits. It's hard to stay in your head when you're struggling to do an intense workout.

I know at some of the most difficult points in my life, exercise was the last thing I wanted to do. It didn't feel important compared to everything else I was dealing with at the time, but whenever I did take the time to work out I was glad I did. The best part about adopting an exercise routine is that it provides a multitude of additional benefits that reach far beyond the centering aspect discussed here.

While I could spend a significant amount of time discussing specific plans and routines that are available, I have not mastered this aspect of my own life and feel unqualified to give a lot of direction. I have, however, added links to some amazing health and fitness coaches on the website for those who are looking for more support in this area.

If you're not currently exercising regularly, just start with walking. It may not make you lose a ton of weight in a short period of time, but walking for twenty minutes a day has a multitude of benefits, including releasing those happy hormones.

STEP 4

Create.

WHEN WE FOCUS
ON WHAT WE WANT,
AND WE FEEL
grateful FOR WHAT
WE'VE ALREADY
BEEN GIVEN, THE
UNIVERSE ALSO
REACTS AND
DELIVERS MORE
THINGS FOR US TO
FEEL GRATEFUL FOR.

STEP 4 - CREATE.
CREATE A CLEAR, EXCITING VISION FOR THE FUTURE

"Life isn't about finding yourself. Life is about creating yourself."
—George Bernard Shaw

Now that we've identified all the seeds of good our transition holds and learned how to center ourselves in the present, it's time to take those seeds and sow them. It's time to plant our garden of greatness, so to speak. Many people struggle in life because they miss this very important step. It's easy to be knocked off course when we don't have a CLEAR vision for where we want to go.

In fact, I would argue that this step is the place where most people fall off course. Why? Because they never had a course to begin with. When we drift aimlessly, it's much easier to get lost. Imagine flying a plane. Did you know that the majority of the time while a plane is in flight it's actually off-course? How do we get from point A to point B if that's the case? Luckily, the pilot is able to course correct, making minor adjustments to the flight path because he knows the exact destination of where he wants to end up. Without the coordinates of his destination, he'd never make it to his landing point successfully.

Life is very similar. Without a clear, detailed vision of EXACTLY where we want to go, we drift aimlessly from one experience to the next. I know this is so true in my own life. At the times I've had a clear picture of my 'Bigger Yes' as I like to call it, I've found it so much easier to say 'no' to things that may seem urgent or important in the short-term but aren't really important to my long-term goals.

I have said 'no' to dessert and felt good about it because I had a long-term goal of losing weight. I've also chosen to say 'yes' too often when I didn't have a long-term goal I was working toward—binge-watching TV shows simply because I didn't have a 'Bigger Yes' to occupy my time or drinking too much because life was feeling boring. Those more aimless decisions left me feeling empty and full of self-loathing. I know I wasn't born to pass my time watching endless amounts of TV or giving into myself every time I want a cookie or a drink, but how easy is it to fall into daily distractions if we don't have a clear and exciting vision of where we're going?

While CREATING A VISION can be one of the most rewarding and fun aspects of the journey through transition, it can also feel overwhelming if you've never thought like this before. It's funny to me how many people—when asked what they want—will rattle off about 10 things they don't want, but they can't clearly articulate what they *do* want. You should try it. Ask some of the people around you to describe exactly what their ideal life would look like five years from now. I'll bet most of you will get a lot of, "Uh... I don't know. Probably just be happy."

When you press them for details like, what does that mean or how will you know if you're really happy, you'll probably find that people get agitated and sometimes even angry trying to answer such deep, hard questions. Why do people have such a hard time with this?

I believe one of the reasons is that we are so conditioned in our society to focus on the negative. This shows up a lot in our daily world as victimhood. Many people feel important and connected to others through talking about their problems and all the reasons life hasn't worked out for them. To step out of this pattern would mean accepting that life, all the good and the bad, is happening FOR us, not TO us. That's bad news if your primary way of relating to others is through the game of WHO HAS THE BIGGEST PROBLEM.

Another reason people often struggle with the CREATING Step is that sometimes we feel selfish when we put our hopes and dreams out into the Universe. We can have the limiting belief that we aren't worthy of our desires and feel guilty for wanting more. It's so important though, to start getting comfortable with not only asking the Universe to provide a way for our desires, but also embracing the gratitude we would feel if those experiences came into our lives.

There is a Universal Law discussed in depth in *The Secret*, also by Rhonda Byrne. The basic premise is that like attracts like. When we focus on what we don't like, or our problems, guess what we get more of? Problems. When we focus on what we want, and we feel grateful for what we've already been given, the Universe also reacts and delivers more things for us to feel grateful for.

Some people struggle with this phase because they've experienced a deep and painful loss, and they feel that moving forward and being happy is in some way betraying the person they lost. If this is you, my advice would be to spend some time in prayer or meditation or whatever space makes you feel more connected to your Higher Power. Ask for peace and the strength to move forward and into a new version of the best life possible. Living a life that is less than your full potential and failing to pursue your dreams will not serve any purpose for the loved one you lost.

One thing that really helped me with combating the feeling of betraying my Dad and moving on was the deep desire to make his life mean something—to become his legacy. I cannot tell you how many times just thinking this way has led me to accomplish things I once thought impossible. We hear stories all the time of parents who start foundations in their child's honor, or who become advocates for causes they become passionate about through their loss. Maybe there is a difference you can make that would HONOR your loved one. Sometimes that's the only place to start during the darkest transitions.

Regardless of the scope of the transitions we face, there are many ways to start creating a CLEAR, EXCITING VISION for our lives. The late Stephen Covey perfectly conveys one of the best ways with his idea from *The 7 Habits of Highly Successful People* to "Begin with the end in Mind." He calls this the rocking chair test (my version is below). Another great way to create a vision is through the process of making a vision board. Goal setting and affirmations also help propel us to an exciting vision for the future. Whichever ways appeal most to you, the goal is to create a BIG, EXCITING YES that drives and motivates you.

MY OWN VERSION OF THE ROCKING CHAIR TEST

Imagine you are a speaker at your own 80th birthday party. Write a speech as though you're going to give a toast to yourself that conveys who you are as a person, what you've stood for in your life and how you've impacted the world in your 80 years. What would you say? Who would be at your party? What vacations would you have taken, experiences would you have had? What themes would be present in your life? Whose lives would you have made a difference in? What would the defining moments of your life look like?

Make sure your speech includes as many details as possible. This is one of the best ways to uncover your guiding values, passions and purpose. After you finish writing your speech, go back and look for any common themes. You may want to write these themes down somewhere because they'll probably be important as you continue to narrow in on your vision for the future both long and short-term.

MAKE A VISION BOARD

A vision board is exactly what it sounds like-a visual representation of your goals and dreams for the future. Not surprisingly it can be especially beneficial for those who have a learning style that favors a visual representation of things. There are no rules or strict guidelines on how to do this, and you can find many examples on the internet. I personally like to include both photos depicting what I want to do, be, and/ or have, and quotes and words that are meaningful to me. Some people scatter their photos all over a poster board, while others like to group their photos by the roles or areas of their lives that makes sense to them.

The important part is to use photos and words that have meaning and illicit feeling for you, and then put it up in a place you will see it every day. I can't tell you how beneficial having a vision board has been for me. I would say next to creating a gratitude practice, it's one of the most important things you can do. It starts your subconscious mind thinking about how to create those experiences and draws you to the things you want far more quickly than you would think possible.

There is one caveat however; you need to be able to start seeing yourself as actually having these things. You need to be able to visualize yourself on that vacation to Europe you've always wanted to take. You need to see yourself becoming the person you would need to become to drive that Range Rover. I've found that it's not about the stuff you will attain through your process of visioning and growth—it's really about who you become in the process. So, when you spend time looking at your vision each day, also spend time thinking about the type of person who can and will achieve their dreams. How will you carry yourself today? How would the person who's achieved these visual goals carry themselves? Feel grateful as though you've already become the person you would need to be to have the life you dream of. It's amazing what the subconscious mind will do to create the reality you seek.

I recommend starting each day by taking about five to ten minutes to look at your vision board. Start visualizing what life would look and feel like and start expressing gratitude to the Universe for providing you that life. Really fully immerse yourself in how living that life would make you feel and choose to feel it now in the present.

For example, if you've gone through a divorce and now have a hard time trusting that you'll find someone new, but you've put a photo of two people who look in love and connected, let go of the feeling that doesn't serve you, and feel the feeling of being loved by and connected to your new spouse. Feel grateful that the Universe knew exactly who to bring you. Feel grateful that your past relationship has helped you feel even more gratitude for the new person in your life. Feel who you've become in the process of letting go of the past relationship and learning to trust again. Feel grateful for the growth and change that have ultimately made you a better and more loving partner.

Another time to use your vision board is when you've had a crummy day or when you feel at your worst, unmotivated and downhearted. I've used the photos that I have on my board to represent my relationship with my husband while we've been in the heat of the moment. This has been a really useful tool for me when I'm at my worst. I try to (and not always successfully) use my vision board when I am down, and I always think to myself, 'How would the person in this photo act?' Would she be more concerned with being right or staying connected? Almost always it leads me to a place where I stop bickering and start sending love and gratitude to my husband. And, what's crazy is many times he'll start responding differently to me too.

I can't stress enough the importance of making and using a vision board daily. It really does catapult your life in the direction of your dreams.

If you'd like resources for creating your vision board, I've included some great resources on www.thrivingthroughtransitions.com.

WITHOUT DEEP *emotional* FEELING ATTACHED TO GOALS, THEY ARE DEAD WORDS THAT WILL GET YOU NOWHERE.

GOAL SETTING

Goal setting is something I look at more as a tool to help move you toward your vision than a method of creating the vision itself, but nonetheless, a very important tool, especially for people like me who tend to look at the big picture and skim over the details. I like to think of a goal as the tool that takes a dream and makes it a reality.

What I mean by that is that without beginning with a clear picture of where you want to go, goals can really just create more work and stress in your life. Goals need to have a 'why' because it's the feelings you associate to your 'why' that will keep you going when times get tough.

I'm reminded of the Simon Sinek quote that explains this idea, "Vision is a destination –a fixed point to which we focus all effort. Strategy is a route–an adaptable path to get us where we want to go."

For example, sometimes people create the goal of running 6 times per week. Then a few weeks into it they start missing days. Why? Because they didn't have a reason or 'why' to begin with, and now, running 6 days per week doesn't feel good anymore. If, however, they set that same goal, but had a vision of competing in a marathon in 6 months, that goal all of a sudden has meaning and value.

Having the big picture in mind also helps us know how to adjust when needed. If the vision is really to be 30 pounds lighter and therefore more confident and happy, the goal of running 6 days per week is just one way to make progress. Then, when running 6 days a week is no longer working, a person can easily change their game plan and create another goal in support of the same vision. Maybe they'll try biking for a while and add in some weights. Maybe they realized they should really be prioritizing their diet more than exercise. The key is to make the goals manageable and connect them to the vision, so they have feelings and meaning attached. Once you have a clear vision you can then start making and tweaking your goals or action plan to achieve it.

I personally like to break my goals down like this:

- What is the overall outcome I am trying to achieve?
- How will I feel if I achieve this?
- What things would I need to accomplish in the next 6 months to move me toward this goal?

- Which of those items can I accomplish in the next month to move me toward this goal?
- Which of those items can I accomplish in the next week?
- Which of those items can I accomplish or work on today?

Sometimes I end up revisiting my 6-month plan and adding to or editing out things that I initially thought would be important.

Here's an easier way to think of it:

End goal/Vision = Strategy (Plan/Sub goals) + Action

If you start to take action, but after a while you aren't getting closer to your end goal, you know you need to make some changes to your strategy.

AFFIRMATIONS

Affirmations are another useful tool when it comes to creating a clear, exciting vision for the future, but they come with the same caution as goal setting. Without deep emotional feeling attached to them, they are dead words that will get you nowhere.

What are affirmations? The dictionary states that to affirm is, "to validate or confirm; to state positively."

Every day we are affirming things to our subconscious mind. Most of the time though, this is an automatic process. If you have an affirmation that says, "I suck at taking tests," and then the next day you fail a math test, you've just affirmed to your subconscious brain that you do indeed suck at taking tests. That's how most people operate. They tell themselves a repetitive, negative story, and then—no surprise—the world serves them up every opportunity to show they are right.

The good news is that affirmations also work in a positive way when we begin to change that internal dialogue. However, if you're normally the kind of person that would focus on all the negative things about yourself, you'll have to work hard to attach meaning and feeling to your affirmations so that they stick.

My advice is to start with just one aspect of yourself that you would like to change.

Create a mental image of what it would feel like to be the person you want to become in that one area.

Let's take health as an example because it's one of the most relatable areas for many people. Say your goal is to lose thirty pounds. What a lot of teachers were originally teaching is to create an affirmation such as, "I, _____, now weigh (*goal weight*)."

Newsflash, this will get you nowhere in a hurry. You know you don't weigh whatever that number is, so basically all you are telling your subconscious brain is, "Not only am I heavy, but I'm also going to lie to myself about it." You haven't done the work to really begin FEELING like the version of you that weighs thirty pounds less.

However, there is great power in the same statement if you attach meaning and feeling to it, "I, _____, now weigh_____, and I feel so ecstatic and thrilled because I am much more confident than I used to be. I enjoy wearing dressy clothes when I go out with friends, and I feel sexy when I'm being intimate with my husband. I really enjoy the active lifestyle that I lead, and I feel inspired to continue being a role model for my family."

What's the difference? Hopefully you can feel the difference in those statements for yourself. In both scenarios you still weigh thirty pounds more than you would like to, but in the second example you start exploring the feelings that you believe you'll feel once you achieve your goal and the subconscious brain recognizes those feelings as real regardless of your current reality. That's the trick. Get your subconscious brain to start feeling the feelings you think you'll have when you get there. It will crave those feelings more and more and your world will start changing to create your new reality. I cannot stress enough, EMOTIONS ARE EVERYTHING!

Personally, I like to take it a step further and write what I like to call GRAFFIRMATIONS, or gratitude-focused affirmations. The basic premise is the same as above, but you'd add in a statement of gratitude for whatever you are affirming as though it's already been done. For example, "I am so incredibly thankful and grateful that I now weigh _____because I feel so ecstatic and thrilled and am so much more confident than I used to be. I feel so grateful that I enjoy wearing dressy clothes when I go out and I feel sexy when my husband and I are intimate together. I also feel blessed that I now lead an active lifestyle and feel inspired to continue being a role model for my family. Thank you, God. Thank you, Universe. Thank you,_____ (whoever you choose to thank)."

As with anything in life, you'll still have to do the work, but gradually you'll start enjoying exercise more, you'll decide you want to eat a little healthier and your brain will crave that comment of how great you're starting to look from your spouse.

Napoleon Hill, one of the most profound thought leaders of all time, has a great quote that says, "Whatever the mind can conceive and believe, the mind can achieve."

I've always taken that to mean that it's not enough to conceive something (affirm it). You must also get yourself to believe it (attach meaning/feeling to it). When you do, it's only a matter of time before it materializes.

Start with only three affirmation statements. Make sure they are clear, exciting, positive focused and FULL OF EMOTION.

WE KNOW
WANT
TO LOOK
SOMETIMES
LIVING
taking
EVERYDAY
IT IS MUCH

WHAT WE
OUR LIVES
LIKE, BUT
ACTUALLY
IT AND
action
TO CREATE
HARDER.

STEP 5

Act.

STEP 5 - ACT.
TAKE INTENTIONAL ACTION

"Sometimes the smallest step in the right direction ends up being the biggest step of your life. Tip toe if you must, but take the step."
—Author Unknown

Even after grieving, getting centered, taking the time to reframe, and creating a new and exciting vision for our future, this may very well be the hardest chapter of the book. Why? Because often we know what we need to do. We know what's good for us. We know what we want our lives to look like, but sometimes actually living it and taking action every day to create it is much harder.

When I was going through my training to become a Certified Transitional Coach I remember my instructor, David Krueger, saying something that really resonated with me on the topic of action. He said, "If knowledge were enough, we'd all be skinny, rich and happy."

Isn't that the truth? Knowledge of what to do isn't enough. We have to take daily action in order to change the course of our lives. Now that we've clearly defined our Point A and Point B, our daily actions must lie on the line between them. Our thoughts will do nothing to actually move us along the path from one place to another. Our thoughts definitely help us clarify both points. Our thoughts help us decide which actions are going to be most beneficial to take, but they don't actually connect the line between the two. We have to do that day-by-day, step-by-step, inch-by-inch.

One of the most motivating YouTube videos that I've watched is of Al Pacino playing

Tony D'Amato in *Any Given Sunday*. In the film he coaches a fictitious struggling football team called the Miami Sharks. One of the pinnacle moments of the movie is Pacino in the locker room giving an inspiring speech about doing the small stuff and taking action:

"I don't know what to say, really. Three minutes till the biggest battle of our professional lives all comes down to today. Now either we heal as a team or we're gonna crumble, inch-by-inch, play-by-play, 'til we're finished.

We're in hell right now, gentlemen, believe me. And, we can stay here–get the shit kicked out of us–or we can fight our way back into the light. We can climb outta hell one inch at a time.

Now, I can't do it for you. I'm too old. I look around. I see these young faces, and I think–I mean–I made every wrong choice a middle-aged man can make. I, uh, I pissed away all my money, believe it or not. I chased off anyone who's ever loved me. And lately, I can't even stand the face I see in the mirror.

You know, when you get old in life things get taken from you. I mean that's...part of life. But, you only learn that when you start losing stuff. You find out life's this game of inches. So is football. Because in either game, life or football, the margin for error is so small–I mean one-half a step too late, or too early, and you don't quite make it. One-half second too slow, too fast, you don't quite catch it.

The inches we need are everywhere around us.

They're in every break of the game, every minute, every second.

On this team, we fight for that inch. On this team, we tear ourselves and everyone else around us to pieces for that inch. We claw with our fingernails for that inch, because we know when we add up all those inches that's gonna make the fuckin' difference between winning and losing! Between livin' and dyin'!

I'll tell you this: In any fight, it's the guy who's willing to die who's gonna win that inch. And I know if I'm gonna have any life anymore, it's because I'm still willin' to fight and die for that inch. Because that's what livin' is! The six inches in front of your face!! Now I can't make you do it. You got to look at the guy next to you. Look into his eyes!

Now I think you're gonna see a guy who will go that inch with you. You're gonna see a guy who will sacrifice himself for this team because he knows, when it comes down to it, you're gonna do the same for him!

That's a team, gentleman!"

The movie goes onto show the team victoriously clinching their conference title and finally overcoming many internal problems.

When you start to think that maybe some action doesn't matter in the big scheme of things, just remember, life is a game of inches. I often times think about this movie when I feel like giving up on my dreams or throwing in the towel.

How do we know which actions to take? In reality, there's no way to know which action is going to create the breakthrough to a new reality, so start by looking at your list of goals and dreams. Make a vision board and look at it daily. What kinds of things would the person you want to become be doing? Start by doing as many of those things as you can.

Let's say that you are working through a painful divorce, but the person you want to become and envision yourself becoming is in a loving and committed relationship. It's not enough to stay at home dreaming of Mr. McDreamy to come whisk you away to live happily ever after. It's not enough to wait around for one of your friends to think of someone who'd be perfect for you. It's not enough to affirm it while staying in every night.

Have you ever heard the saying, "You may have to kiss a few frogs before you find Prince Charming?" Well, it's true. You may have to put yourself out there, maybe join a dating site, maybe try speed dating, but whatever you do, do something that moves you toward the life you want.

Maybe none of the men you meet will end in happily ever after, but you'll learn and grow so much along the way. Businesses understand this really well. Sometimes you have to fail a few times before you find the magic solution to your problems, but nobody ever gets there without taking action.

Shortly after my Dad died I was at a complete and utter loss for how to move forward with my life. Looking back on the 6 months or so after he died I have very vague memories of what I even did. I was stuck, and I knew it. I decided it was time to seek some professional help because I wasn't doing so great on my own. I had become a zombie, going through the motions without any direction, drive, or purpose.

After 'kissing a few frogs' (I tried a few therapists who were under-qualified to say the least) I finally met a therapist who understood my dilemma. By that point I had also identified that I needed someone to challenge me to take action, so right up front I told him, "I want you to just tell what to do. I don't care if you tell me the wrong thing. I don't care if I have to try 10 different things to help me start living again. I just want you to keep telling me what to do next."

After our first session he suggested that I go down into the room in my house that my Dad had been staying in. He said for now I was just to sit there, surrounded by his things and take it all in.

Seemed like a pretty insignificant action item, but at this point I was desperate. I did what he asked, and amazingly I felt a little of the fog start to lift.

The next week when we met he gave me a new action item. He wanted me to pick out a few of his belongings to keep, give my siblings the same opportunity, and the rest I was to donate.

I wasn't sure I was ready for this step, but I wanted to get through this pain that I was wallowing in, so I decided I would do as I was told. After all, that was what I had asked for.

I began that very night sifting through all of his belongings—the Tommy Bahama shirts that still smelled like his cologne, the New York Yankees jacket that he bought on one of his trips to Las Vegas—it was all an agonizing reminder that he was truly gone. At first, I wanted to keep most of it. I didn't want to let it go, but in reality, my Dad was a big guy, and it wasn't going to fit any of us.

Finally, I came to terms with the reality that all of his things were just things without his larger-than-life personality to fill them. I put most of the items in bags and took them downtown to a non-profit group I knew would hand them out to those in need as winter approached.

WHAT KINDS OF THINGS WOULD THE PERSON YOU WANT TO BECOME BE DOING? START BY *doing* AS MANY OF THOSE THINGS AS YOU CAN.

That was a hard day. Interestingly enough though, the fog began to clear a little more. From that point on I felt like I could handle life again. I no longer felt like a zombie. I had bad days and good days, but at least I was living again.

Sometimes taking action is really just as simple as choosing to go sit with your pain for a while. Sometimes it requires a lot more effort than that. The great thing though is that action usually begets action. So, even if the first action you take ends up being a 'frog' that's okay. You'll have more and more opportunities to take action the more you practice doing it, and I can almost guarantee that one of those actions will eventually move you forward on your path to Point B.

If you're someone like me, and you don't know where to start or are afraid to take action because it may be the wrong one, here are some ideas that you might want to try:

Create a list of 30 possible actions you could take – Each day for 30 days try one of those action items. When something works, think of the next thing you could do to take action in that same direction and then the next day do that.

If you're really stuck, go for a walk – Tony Robbins often talks about how motion creates emotion, so if you're feeling dead inside, one of the best things you can do is begin a habit of walking. I've had so many of my best ideas come to me when I've been on a walk.

Go back to getting centered – Sometimes we need to quiet the busyness of our lives and the best action we can take is going back to centering ourselves in the present moment. It may not seem like a big action step, but it helps immensely.

Work on building a new habit – about a year ago I started the habit of making my bed every day after hearing Gretchen Rubin talk about it on her podcast, Happier. There's a day here and there that I've missed, but I can't tell you what that one seemingly meaningless habit has done for me and my overall happiness. Sometimes we need to simply make room for more positive habits in our daily routine.

Do one thing different – this could look as simple as exchanging your tunes for a podcast instead. There is actually a great book by Bill O'Hanlon called, *Do One Thing Different* that talks about why this method for achievement works so well, but simply changing out one part of your daily routine can make big impacts over the long haul. I highly recommend reading this book if this concept appeals to you.

Fail forward – Maybe the last action step you took was a complete and utter failure. That's ok. In fact, that's largely the path to success. Transitions are tough. They aren't going to be perfect. You're essentially learning a new way of life, so expect to fail. Even most of the greatest achievers of our time have failed more times than they could count. Failure is part of the game, but as I've often said during my thirteen years of coaching volleyball, "Fail in a different way. Make a new mistake. Fail forward."

I hope these ideas inspire you to take action and start moving forward on your path to Point B, but I also know inspiration isn't enough. If it was, you'd already be thriving. That's why, I believe, the single best action you can take is creating your support and accountability system through hiring a coach, finding an accountability partner or even joining a mastermind or group coaching.

Any of these options provides ongoing encouragement and external pressure to work toward your Point B.

HIRE A COACH OR COUNSELOR

I've worked with several life coaches over the years, and I can honestly say that committing time and resources to working with a professional guide is one of the best decisions I've ever made. Ten years ago, when my Dad passed away there weren't a lot of professionals in this field yet, so I sought out a counselor, but had I known more about coaching I would have hired a coach instead. Don't get me wrong, counselors definitely have their place, but what I love about coaching is that it's usually much more action oriented, as well as future focused.

Whether a person is looking to develop healthier habits, looking to unlock their personal potential or they are just looking to identify their new, exciting vision, a personal coach can help cultivate actual results.

Life coaching is an umbrella term that is used by those in the industry to describe the many areas in which a coach can help you. From career development to a balanced life, from fulfillment to THRIVING through your transitions, a life coach will know what questions to ask you based on where you currently are. This means that a life coach can help almost anyone.

Developing the best life possible requires clarity, growth and passion. The number one benefit of hiring a life coach is the motivation that comes from working with someone who is invested in you. This passionate energy will help boost your confidence and allow you to release any negative energy that you are holding onto. This will allow you to make clearer decisions in your day to day life that will put you on the right track towards success.

In addition to providing you with insight, a life coach will stand by you and support you through your toughest times and will help celebrate your successes as you achieve them. It is important to acknowledge the obstacles that you overcome, and having someone to share these accomplishments with will empower you and help you create momentum. This momentum can help in every area of your life.

Just remember, you may find that you have to 'kiss a few frogs' before finding the right coach for you. If you end up deciding to try coaching my suggestion is that you do some research. Read through stories or blog posts from potential coaches, read their bios, get to know them as much as you can. Many coaches will offer a free consultation. I recommend scheduling a few and then deciding if one coaches style resonates with you best.

Of course, I would love to work with you if you're seriously committed to THRIVING through your transition, but I'm not the perfect fit for everyone—and I know that. I take on a limited number of one-on-one coaching clients each quarter, and I'm committed to working with people who are ready to do whatever it takes to successfully navigate the changes they're facing. In any case, feel free to schedule a complimentary coaching session on the website. If I can't help you personally, I'm happy to direct you to another coach who I feel might be a good fit.

FIND AN ACCOUNTABILITY PARTNER

This is another (often free) option that works really well for some people. However, it's best to follow some strict guidelines:

Schedule regular check-ins – One of the reasons people often fail at having an accountability partner is because they don't hold themselves accountable for scheduling regular meetings with their accountability partner. It's always best to determine how often you'll meet as partners before you begin working with someone.

Set clear guidelines – One thing that derails the success of working with an accountability partner the fastest is when your meeting turns into social hour. Avoid this by setting clear guidelines for your meetings. How long will the meeting last? How will the time be used? Where will the meeting take place? The more that you can set clearly defined guidelines for your accountability relationship the greater your chances are of success.

Choose an acquaintance, or even a stranger, over a friend – Don't choose someone who is super close to you to be your accountability partner. This can lead to inaction very quickly for multiple reasons. First, when you choose someone you're very comfortable with it's much easier for either side to blow off their commitments because they know that their partner will be understanding. Secondly, it's much easier for the relationship to turn to social connection time, which is great, but not very productive. Lastly, it's sometimes harder for a person who is close to you and cares about you to provide the honesty you sometimes need from an accountability partner.

Choose only 1-3 actions to work on together. By choosing just a few actions to focus on, you'll have a far greater chance for success and it will be much easier for your partner to help hold you accountable.

Think about hiring an accountability partner. I've heard of a few people that offer this. It's similar to coaching, but not as in depth and more specific to action items you set.

JOIN A MASTERMIND

I absolutely LOVE masterminds and I attribute some amazing successes to the masterminds I've been a part of. Mastermind groups are a great way to access accountability and support and they can also provide inspiration and motivation.

Some masterminds are all peer to peer interactions, and everyone takes turns leading the group, while other masterminds are led by a coach who takes the group through a specific set of objectives – more like group coaching. Both can be extremely effective if done right.

I love masterminds so much that I've developed an amazing program called the THRIVE TOGETHER MASTERMIND, specifically focused on providing support, education, accountability and action items around the Steps of *Thriving Through Transitions*. Each session lasts 90 days and is limited to 20 members. For more information go to www. thrivingthroughtransitions.com/thrive-together/.

Whether you choose to be a part of the THRIVE TOGETHER MASTERMIND, or you choose to find a different one or create your own, make sure it addresses the following:

There is an agenda – For mastermind groups to be successful there needs to be a clear agenda for each meeting. Similar to working with an accountability partner, there should be specific guidelines for every meeting including how long each person has to share, whether or not there is a theme or focus area for the meeting, how the members will support each other, whether or not there will be lessons on different topics pertaining to the group, etc.

There is a common thread – I personally believe it's really important to identify a common thread within the group. Whether it's that all the members are entrepreneurs, or everyone is working on overcoming addiction, or everyone went to the same seminar, or enjoyed the same book–find at least one common thread that ties the group together. It will help create intimacy and connection, and it helps identify the purpose of the group.

Everyone is invested – There is something that happens when a person makes a financial commitment to something. I HIGHLY recommend making sure everyone is financially invested in the mastermind group because typically people are more likely to keep their commitments when they've put some skin in the game. I'm not saying it has to be thousands of dollars, but making everyone commit financially will have a significant impact on the overall commitment of the group. If there aren't any costs associated to the group, you could always just ask everyone to donate some amount to a local charity to show their commitment level.

There is a set timeline – I recommend that masterminds regularly have opportunities for members to evaluate their commitment to the group. Personally, I think 90 days is the perfect timing for groups to evaluate whether or not the group is still adding value to its members. Some groups stay together for decades while others part ways after only a few months. By giving people the chance to reevaluate their commitment to the group on a quarterly, half-yearly or yearly basis, members will continue to feel like they GET to be a part of the group rather than HAVE to. There is nothing worse than feeling like you have one more item on your to-do list that you don't want to do.

There is a screening process - The screening process helps identify the common thread of the group and the commitment level of each potential member. For masterminds to be successful it's usually important that the members are true peers. If there isn't a very level playing field some members won't feel like they are getting enough value from the group or can feel like they are becoming more of a mentor to other members rather than a peer.

On the flip side, members who don't feel as successful or knowledgeable can feel less confident to make recommendations or give their opinions and it can lead to some members feeling inferior or bad about themselves (the exact opposite of what we'd want to happen).

Sometimes having a coach or leader in the group is helpful because they remind the group of their common thread and act as a moderator - involving all members of the group and making sure they feel supported and engaged.

Celebrations happen regularly - In mastermind groups, and also in life, we need to celebrate our successes! It's so easy to get caught up in our desire for more and better, that we often times forget to stop and celebrate and enjoy life!

There is also something beautiful that happens when we celebrate the successes of others. Our society often conditions us to think that another's success is a negative thing—that there's only so much room for successful, fulfilled people, and their success equals your failure—which, of course, is total B.S. Masterminds are a great place to celebrate and enjoy the successes of everyone! It feels so natural within the intimacy of the group, and it's so empowering to feel the reciprocation of the group celebrating your successes.

Masterminds are a great way to access the power of collective synergy. Often times, they are also a less expensive alternative to one-on-one coaching that can produce similar results. Just make sure you find a group that you feel connected to and resonate with, and that it addresses the professional aspects outlined above.

JOIN THE THRIVING THROUGH TRANSITIONS COMMUNITY

I've also created a place for people to come together and support each other through their transitions online. This is a place for people to share the actions they are taking, ask for support and offer helpful and specific solutions to the tough challenges transitions often bring. You can find a link to the Facebook group, *Thriving Through Transitions Community*, on our website: www.thrivingthroughtransitions.com.

The only thing I ask is that, if you join this community of fellow Thrivers, you commit to posting what you are doing each day for the first 30 days to move through your transition. You can look at it as an accountability group. Plus, by taking an action every day, you'll start to build momentum toward your new life.

TAKE ACTION TODAY

Another thing that is extremely important is to take action NOW. Not tomorrow, not later on today, but right now. What is the simplest action you can take right now to move you through your transition? Could you write a letter to yourself? Maybe a letter to someone else? Maybe it would be good to just go for a walk? Maybe make yourself a profile on a dating site? Maybe apply for a job without the intention of even getting it?

A good place to start is the thing that scares you the most about your transition. In my example, by getting rid of my Dad's things, I felt like I was finally saying, "He really is gone. He's not coming back." It may seem stupid that removing his things was one of the catalysts I needed to move forward, but his things to me were a metaphor. They were my way of trying to control the situation, which was clearly out my control. They were the evidence that maybe somehow this was all just a nightmare that I'd eventually be able to wake up from. They were the daily reminder of pain and agony that seemed to have become my life.

SOMETIMES
WE GET SO
CAUGHT UP IN
OUR DAY TO DAY
feelings THAT WE
SABOTAGE OUR
TRANSITIONS
BECAUSE WE
DON'T FEEL
LIKE ACTING
DIFFERENTLY
THAT DAY.

In my divorce, one of the actions I was able to take was in preparation for what I knew would be coming. I had been staying at home with my kids, but knew that I would need to start making money if I was ever going to get out of the situation I was in. I decided to go back to work so that I could eventually leave my marriage. It was hard to take my kids to daycare. I never saw myself doing that. I always wanted to be like my mom, a person I greatly respect and admire, and be a homemaker raising my children, but I knew I needed to give up that dream (at least for the time being) to be able to end my marriage. And then, guess what? I'm right back to square one grieving the loss of an idealistic view of what my life could have been.

The beauty of taking the first step is that you start moving, even if it feels like a tip toe, toward Point B, and by embracing the change, you often end up in an even better situation than you could have imagined. I went back to work for a couple of years, and it was really hard, but then I met my husband. When we moved in together, we had space to set up a salon in our home, so I was able to work from home, make my own hours, AND be home with our kids. If I'd never taken that first step though, who knows what would have happened? I fully believe that the Universe supports and rewards people as they step into their truth and start taking action to support themselves, so I know it's no accident that my life has continued to become more amazing and magical as I've learned and grown and taken ACTION toward my dreams, even if sometimes it's felt more like I'm doing a little Cha-Cha (two steps forward, one step back) rather than a sprint.

Let's look at your transition now. Hopefully you've already begun the process of CREATING your dream life on paper. Now, it's time to start acting on those dreams.

"The distance between your dreams and reality is called ACTION."
—Unknown

What action/actions am I committed to taking TODAY to THRIVE no matter where I am at in my transition? What is one small step I can tangibly start with RIGHT NOW, with the resources I already have, that will move me toward Point B?

_____

_____

_____

_____

_____

_____

_____

_____

Why is right now the perfect time to take this step? How will this action help me THRIVE and why am I 100% committed to taking this action?

_____

_____

_____

_____

_____

_____

_____

Another important consideration are the actions that you should *quit doing* because you know they are holding you back. Sometimes these include reminding yourself daily of your loss through watching videos or looking at pictures. Sometimes it's getting together with your girlfriends and talking about how horrible your husband was to you for the 50th time. Sometimes it's slandering your employer because you were fired even though deep inside you knew you weren't giving it all you could. Sometimes it's shutting the world out and avoiding people because you don't want to have to move forward.

A few weeks after my Dad died I remember my Mom came over to my house. I'd been pretty depressed, and she could definitely tell. I still remember her having one of those 'tough love' conversations with me that day. She said, "Jocelyn, it's time to pull yourself out of this funk. You get a day to feel really crappy every once in a while, but after that you need to get up and handle life and be the Mom your kids need you to be. If that means that you cry your heart out at night once your kids are asleep, that's fine. But from the time you wake up to the time you go to bed, you need to get busy living!"

I can't remember where I heard it, but I once heard someone ask on a podcast or radio show I was listening to why there was such a rise in depression in recent years when most of us actually live better than the wealthiest people in the world did even a few centuries ago. I remember the response because it really struck a chord for me. The man responded that prior to industrial revolution people simply didn't have the luxury of time to sit around thinking about their mental health or their problems because meeting the physical demands of their work and providing the basics for their families took up the majority of their time and energy.

I think there is something great we can learn from our ancestors here. Sometimes we get so caught up in our day to day feelings that we sabotage our transitions because we don't feel like acting differently that day. We feel like wallowing in self-pity, and unfortunately, society also rewards us for it. If it helps, remind yourself of that awesome phrase that accompanies the infamous Nike swoosh symbol, "Just do it." Whether you feel like it or not, get up out of your misery and live. Stop feeling sorry for yourself, stop eating crappy food if you want to lose weight, stop making excuses or blaming people for things, and stop talking about all your problems.

I love the quote from Rita Shiano, "Talking about problems is our greatest addiction." Isn't that the truth? If you ever want to make a room go silent fast, start talking about how great your life is. Seriously. It totally freaks most people out because we are so conditioned by society that *he who has the biggest problem is the most important.*

I know deeply ingrained habits are hard to change. I struggle with this all the time. I know I shouldn't speak badly of anyone, but out of hurt or pain or whatever lame reason, I sometimes have, and guess what? I almost always feel like I'm taking one of those Cha-Cha steps in the wrong direction.

This is why making the choice to stop destructive patterns is another important way we can take action toward our Point B.

What are my most destructive patterns regarding my transition? Do I blame or criticize? Do I seek attention through talking about my problems? Do I avoid people who I know would challenge me or give me 'tough love'?

_____

_____

_____

_____

_____

_____

_____

_____

_____

How can I combat these negative patterns? What will I do differently when I feel myself starting to fall back into them? What can I commit to STOP doing right now TODAY?

_____

_____

_____

_____

_____

_____

_____

Afterward

THAT LINE —
THE MESSY
LINE THAT
CONNECTS
POINT A AND
POINT B —
THAT'S WHERE
THE *growth*
TAKES PLACE.

AFTERWARD

"The secret of change is to focus all of your energy, not on fighting the old, but on building the new." —Socrates

Transitions are fluid and messy. They aren't the calm easy days that come when you finally hit Point B, but you wouldn't appreciate the mountain top without the climb. That line—the messy line that connects Point A and Point B—that's where the growth takes place. Without that line we'd have no opportunity to discover our greatness. Without that line, we'd be stuck in an eternity of pain—no way to transition, grow, learn and change—and that's where the magic of life happens.

If you haven't gone through and completed the different questions and Steps of THRIVING, I'd highly encourage you to go back through the book now and DO THE WORK. While I love being able to share my story and feel immense gratitude for you choosing to take the time to be here with me, the real magic of your transition lies in your own answers to the tough questions and your daily actions toward your future. INVEST IN YOURSELF. Whether through some of the suggestions outlined in this book or by listening to your own inner wisdom. My only hope is that you start the journey of using your transition to THRIVE.

I'd love to connect with you directly and support you through your journey in any way I can. Truly, my passion and purpose in life is fulfilled through creating meaningful connections with the people I'm blessed to meet and know. Please feel free to email me at jocelyn@jocelynkuhn.com and I'll be sure to respond. I'd love to know your story, and I greatly appreciate your support of mine.

I leave you with this quote by Cheryl Strayed, "You don't have a right to the cards you believe you should have been dealt. You have an obligation to play the hell out of the ones you're holding."

We were put on this earth not just to experience all the beautiful parts of life, but to also experience the painful parts. That's how we learn empathy and compassion. That's how we grow and make our transformation. We aren't promised days without pain, but we can still choose to THRIVE through those difficult times in life. Through accepting grief as part of the process, finding the good in all things, learning to be present, and creating and living the best version of our life we can live, we will THRIVE.

NOTES

DEFINING YOUR TRANSITION

Transition. (n.d.). Retrieved February 15, 2017, from https://www.merriam-webster. com/dictionary/transition

Step 1 – GRIEVE

Harrison, Vicki. "A Quote by Vicki Harrison." *Goodreads*, Goodreads, 2012, www. goodreads.com/quotes/543175-grief-is-like-the-ocean-it-comes-on-waves-ebbing.

Axelrod, J. (2016). The 5 Stages of Grief & Loss. *Psych Central*. Retrieved on February 16, 2017, from https://psychcentral.com/lib/the-5-stages-of-loss-and-grief/

Kübler-Ross, Elisabeth. On Death and Dying. The Macmillan Company, 1969.

Step 2 – REFRAME

Hillenbrand, Laura. *Unbroken: A World War II Story of Survival, Resilience, and Redemption.* New York: Random House, 2010. Print.

Campbell, Joseph, et al. *The Hero's Journey: the World of Joseph Campbell: Joseph Campbell on His Life and Work.* Harper & Row, 1990.

Step 3 – CENTER

Byrne, Rhonda. *The Magic.* Simon and Schuster, 2012.

Step 4 – CREATE

Byrne, Rhonda. *The Secret.* New York: Hillsboro, Ore.: Atria Books, 2006.

Covey, Stephen. *The 7 Habits of Highly Effective People.* Simon & Schuster, 1999.

Kuhn, Greg. *How Quantum Physicists Build New Beliefs: Your Personal Coaching Guide to Truly and Fully Unleash the Law of Attraction.* CreateSpace, 2013.

"Affirm." *Merriam-Webster.com.* Merriam-Webster, n.d. Web. 30 May 2018.

Step 5 – ACT

Stone, Oliver, director. *Any given Sunday.* 1999.

AFTERWARD NOTES

Strayed, Cheryl. *Tiny Beautiful Things: Advice on Love and Life from Someone Who's Been There.* Atlantic, 2013.

Made in the USA
San Bernardino, CA
02 July 2018